"It's been a long time since I've read a parenting book that was more enjoyable than this one. Robert Wolgemuth's helpful advice coupled with his humor and transparency is wonderful. Once you start reading, it will be hard to put the book down."

GARY SMALLEY
Author

"With a five-year-old daughter, I needed advice, wisdom, and direction. I found it in She Calls Me Daddy. Robert Wolgemuth has provided me and other dads with the godly wisdom to raise godly daughters."

STEPHEN ARTERBURN
Cofounder and Chairman of Minirth Meier
New Life Clinics

"As a clinical psychologist, I can assure you that Robert Wolgemuth's counsel is sound. As a theologian, I can affirm that his approach is solid. This book is filled with profound truth, practical ideas, and it's great fun to read. What a wonderful combination!"

RODNEY L. COOPER, PH.D.
National Director for Education
Promise Keepers

"One of the greatest advantages I have had in life is being well-loved by my father. If he were alive today, he would agree wholeheartedly with this book. By practicing these principles, he gave my sister and me a foundation of love and confidence that nothing can shake."

DALE HANSON BOURKE
Publisher, Religion News Service

"If you knew this man's daughters like I know this man's daughters, you would buy this book, read it carefully, and do exactly as it says. You would also give a copy to every man you know who's raising a daughter."

MARK DEVRIES
Author, *Family-Based Youth Ministry*

"You want advice on raising daughters from someone who has done it. Robert Wolgemuth and his wife, Bobbie, have done it. I know their daughters, and you need look no further for examples. If you have a daughter, this is the right book for you."

JERRY B. JENKINS
Author

She Calls Me *Daddy*

ROBERT WOLGEMUTH

TYNDALE

Tyndale House Publishers, Wheaton, Illinois

to
Melissa Christine Wolgemuth Schrader
and Julie Elizabeth Wolgemuth

Library of Congress Cataloging-in-Publication Data

Wolgemuth, Robert D.

    She calls me daddy/by Robert D. Wolgemuth
       p. cm.
    ISBN 1-56179-652-2
    1. Fathers and daughters. 2. Parenting. 3. Fatherhood—Religious aspects—
Christianity. 4. Conduct of life. I. Title.
HQ756.W65   1996
307.874'2—dc20   96-2303
                                               CIP

A Focus on the Family book published by
Tyndale House Publishers, Wheaton, Illinois 60189

Unless otherwise noted, Scripture quotations are from the HOLY BIBLE, NEW INTER-
NATIONAL VERSION. ® Copyright © 1973, 1978, 1984 by the International Bible Society. Used by permission of Zondervan Publishing House. All rights reserved. Quotations identified NASB are from the New American Standard Bible, © 1960, 1963, 1968,
1971, 1973, 1975, and 1977 by The Lockman Foundation. Used by permission.

People's names and certain details of the case studies in this book have been changed to
protect the privacy of the individuals involved. However, the facts of what happened
and the underlying principles have been conveyed as accurately as possible.

Editor: Larry K. Weeden
Front cover design: The Puckett Group, Atlanta, Georgia.

Printed in the United States of America

99 00 01 02 03 04/11 10 9 8 7 6 5 4 3 2 1

Contents

Acknowledgments vii

Foreword *by Gary Smalley* xi

Preface *by Missy Wolgemuth Schrader* xiii
 and Julie Wolgemuth

Introduction xv

PART ONE Someone Who Calls You "Daddy"

Chapter One What's a Nice Guy Like You Doing 3
 in a Book Like This?

Chapter Two Hanging in There 19
 Sure I Can Finish This Today

PART TWO Never Too Tough, Never
 Too Tender—Seven Things
 You Must Know

Chapter Three Protection 33
 Able to Leap Tall Buildings
 in a Single Bound

Chapter Four Conversation 55
 Just Keep Talking

Chapter Five Affection 79
 Daddy, Hold Me

Chapter Six   **Discipline**   101
                       A Sledgehammer, a Couple of
                       Crowbars, and a Level

Chapter Seven   **Laughter**   121
                       Did You Hear the One About . . . ?

Chapter Eight   **Faith**   141
                       Jesus Loves Me, This I Know

Chapter Nine   **Conduct**   161
                       You Be the Judge

PART THREE   **Gentlemen, We Have Our**
                       Assignments

Chapter Ten   **A Quick Look Inside**   193
                       The Guy from the City Inspector's
                       Office

Afterword   **A Chapter for Special Dads**   205
                       Stepdads, Long-Distance Dads,
                       and Single Dads

                       Questions for Discussion   215

Acknowledgments

There's nothing a man has that hasn't been given to him. I know this because I'm such a man.

My parents, Sam and Grace Wolgemuth, made me the envy of nearly all my friends. "I just love your parents" is something I've heard from the time I was a small boy right up to the present. Together they represent absolute toughness, tenderness, and godliness.

The influence of my five siblings—Ruth, Sam, Ken, Debbie, and Dan—helped to shape me before I knew it. Their love and support today are as accessible as a daily download from the Internet. Their spouses and children have also had a substantial impact on my life.

This book never would have been possible without Bobbie, the wife of my youth. Her love gave me the ability to believe in myself. Her creativity, laughter, and wisdom became the substance of our home. And her friendship and encouragement give me a boatload of anticipation for tomorrow's adventures.

I deeply appreciate the tender relationship Bobbie had—and still has—with her dad, Dr. Ray Gardner. That allowed her to trust in me and enthusiastically support my connection with our daughters.

Our daughters, Missy and Julie, have hung in with their amateur dad from the time he made his first mistake with them until now. I am ever grateful for their patience during the early years and for their friendship today as grown-ups.

I'm thankful, too, for our son-in-law, Jon Schrader, a gift to our daughter and the whole family. And now that God has blessed Jon with Abigail Grace, a little girl of his own, the fun of being the father of a daughter continues to the next generation.

The two Sunday school classes I've had the privilege of teaching—"The New Horizons" in Waco and "The Adventure Class" in Nashville—will never know what their love and support have meant. My thanks go to them for the chance they've given me to stand in front of them, listening for God's clear voice in *my* life.

I also want to acknowledge my agent and friend, Steve Brallier from the William Morris Agency, and the wonderful people at Focus on the Family Publishing—Dean Merrill, Al Janssen, Larry Weeden, Ray Pokorny, Lorraine Beck, Mike Leming, Melanie Beroth, Kathi Allen, Robin Brink, Tammi Scheetz, Amy Jo Riester, Shirley Neeley, Connie Carleton, Meg Goad, Yvette Mihaly—and their boss, Dr. James Dobson, who didn't stop bugging me about this book until it was finished.

Thanks go as well to my old friends at The Puckett Group for their unmistakable touch on the book's cover design.

Thanks to Gary and Norma Smalley for their friendship, and to Gary for his willingness to write the foreword.

You wouldn't be reading this book if not for the sales team at Nelson/Word Publishing, which has been given the task of delivering this book to the marketplace. So many of those people are friends and former colleagues. I'm grateful for the diligent efforts of each one.

Mike Hyatt has been my business partner for many years. It was on a long drive from Hilton Head Island with Bobbie, Mike, and his wife, Gail, that the idea of a book for dads with daughters really took form—the Hyatts have five daughters! I will always be grateful for Mike's faithful support and friendship during the good years and, especially, the tough ones.

To Doug and Gay Shumaker, thanks for allowing Bobbie and me

to hide away in your "cabin in the South Carolina woods" to write this book.

I'm also grateful to the nine dads who carefully read the manuscript, told me what they really thought, and made many helpful suggestions: Ron Perry, Don White, Gary Baird, Mark DeVries, Dale Jamison, George Yowell, Neil Newton, Allen Kennedy, and Ron Bargatze.

And to those who, over the years, have challenged, encouraged, and prayed with and for me and my family, your friendship has been a priceless gift. Thanks to each one.

Foreword

There's no challenge for a man quite like being the father of a girl. My challenge began in 1967 when Kari was born. Two years later, our first son was born, and three years after that came our second son. So as it turned out, Kari, our firstborn, was our only daughter.

Having spent my childhood as an unusually adventurous boy, I had no idea what to expect in the challenging experience of raising a girl. What I discovered as Kari grew was this: Girls are wonderful *and* very different from boys!

Boys often love to be tousled and teased by their dads. Girls love to be cherished. Boys can be "spoken to" with single words, half sentences, and grunts. Girls want their dads to talk to them in complete sentences. Boys long to live without their dad's protection. Most girls thrive with confidence when they know their dad will be there.

This is a book about three important issues that dads with daughters need to understand: Honor, boundaries, and balance. As I read the book you now hold in your hands, I couldn't help but be impressed with the importance honor plays—a dad taking time to honor his daughter with his love and his time, teaching her to honor and respect him, then helping her understand the importance of honoring God and others.

This book also gives dads a clear understanding of the importance of building solid fences—border lines to instruct and protect a girl.

When I was a youngster, I learned a lesson about the importance of heeding boundaries. I lived in a home where there were no boundaries, so I had concluded that border lines and restrictions were there to disrupt my life, not protect it.

Crawling through the barbed-wire fence at Boulder Flats one day, a friend and I discovered that the huge rocks covering an innocent-looking, dry riverbed housed hundreds of rattlesnakes. Lucky to have escaped with my life, I came to realize that boundaries are essential.

This is a book about building healthy, self-worth-enhancing boundaries for your daughter. However, unlike the simple "Keep Out" signs at Boulder Flats, this book carefully explains why such boundaries are so important to build and guard.

Finally, this is a book about balance. Tenderness and discipline. Crisis and laughter. Teaching and learning. Honesty and fairness. Protection and freedom. It's a book that will help you to actually *be* a better father to your daughter. And don't worry—it's filled with lots of practical ideas so you'll know exactly what to do.

If you're looking for a book to help you accomplish your goal of teaching honor, building boundaries, and creating balance, this is it.

The message of *She Calls Me Daddy* is clear: Whoever you are, however long ago your daughter was born, whatever your background or your current situation, you can be a *great* daddy.

One more thing. There are lots of good parenting books out there filled with helpful recommendations. I've read many of them. I've even written some! But it has been a long time since I've read a parenting book that was more enjoyable than this one. Robert Wolgemuth's helpful advice, coupled with his humor and transparency, is wonderful. Once you start reading, it will be hard to put the book down.

You're in for a treat.

GARY SMALLEY
Branson, Missouri

Preface

You can imagine the fun we both had the first time we read our dad's manuscript for this book. We laughed out loud remembering the stories of our growing-up years.

But what was so interesting was reading the reasons behind some of the things Daddy did with us. As children, we experienced the "what" every day, but in reading this book, we learned the "why." It was really interesting to look at our dad's "strategy" in being our dad—kind of like seeing how a watch works after having spent a lifetime just telling time.

As kids, we had the fun of spending the night with lots of our friends. One of the things we realized was that no two families are exactly alike. Happy families come in many shapes and sizes. Some of what you're about to read will work well in your home, just as it did in ours, and some things will need your own personalization.

But, simple as this might sound, there's one important thing we discovered about other families: Some of our friends were able to talk to their dads, and some weren't.

The most important thing in this book is the chapter on conversation. Of all the things our dad taught us, we're most thankful for his conversation "lessons." As we grew up, our friends often asked in amazement, "You told your dad *that?*" Our ability to talk with him about our lives and how we really felt has built a bond that's the foundation of our friendship with him today.

We truly hope this book is helpful to you and your daughter, just as its principles were to us.

Oh, by the way, Daddy, that navy sweater we borrowed from you five years ago is probably in the cheerleaders' lost-and-found closet at Brentwood Academy.

MISSY WOLGEMUTH SCHRADER AND JULIE WOLGEMUTH

Introduction

Although it was only 10:15 at night, the ringing of our nightstand telephone woke Bobbie and me from a sound sleep. Some say that "first" sleep is the deepest, and, as our friends will tell you, if our daughters are safely home, phone calls after 9:30 will probably wake us up!

The phone wakes me in a flash. Unless they're wrong numbers, rarely do late-night calls contain any coincidental information.

The caller was Missy, our older daughter. She was a freshman in college, and that night, no matter how late it was, she needed me. So, sitting cross-legged on the floor just in front of the nightstand on Bobbie's side of the bed, I listened to her story.

The guy she was describing was Mitch, a senior. He and Missy had been dating for several weeks, and they had enjoyed their time together. But something had gone wrong, at least from Missy's vantage point. Mitch had decided that Missy was to be his wife. He was sure of it. And his parents, whom she had met the weekend before, were also satisfied that Mitch had found "Miss Right."

I could hear the panic in Missy's voice. "I like Mitch, I really do," she said. "He's a nice boy and everything. But marriage? Not now. Not to Mitch. No way!"

Her voice dropped and she asked, "Dad, what should I do? I'm really scared."

We talked for about an hour. There were some tears . . . and some laughing. I asked her a lot of questions, "thought out loud" with her, and offered the advice she had called for—the best I could give. We exchanged mutual "I love you's" and "Good night's."

By the time I crawled back into bed, Bobbie was asleep. Unable to do battle with the sandman, she had decided to wait until morning to get the lowdown. Unfortunately, I wasn't as lucky. So, for what may have been an hour, I lay there thinking about Missy and the phone call.

I remember feeling overwhelmed with emotion, awestruck at what had just happened. Our daughter was trying out her freshman-in-college independence. Just down the hall, except for some high school memorabilia still on the walls, her bedroom was empty. Technically, she didn't live here anymore. But apparently still trusting her dad's advice, she had called me for help.

"What a wonderful gift you have given me tonight, Missy," I whispered out loud. "Thank you."

The next morning over coffee, Bobbie and I talked about the call, every single detail—at least those I could remember. We refer to this kind of thorough report as "the woman's version." And I told her about my thoughts after the call and my gratitude.

In the next few minutes, we began a conversation that has continued for several years. That conversation has, in fact, led to this book. We've discussed what had happened when Missy was a little girl that gave her the confidence to call home for more than a little extra spending money. Why did she trust my advice? And why, as we learned later, did she take it?

Bobbie and I both had the luxury of growing up in solid, Christian homes. Most of our growing-up memories are good. Some of what we did with our girls was similar to what we had seen our parents do, and some of it has been quite different.

Because I've been professionally connected to the publishing industry for more than 20 years, we've been surrounded by helpful magazine articles and books of every description, and some of what we've done as parents came from them.

We've also had the privilege of attending several helpful seminars and workshops. There are things we've done with our daughters that we can recall some of those teachers suggesting.

Although some of the information in this book did come from our parents, books, and helpful experts, most of what has happened in the past 25 years has come as a result of a simple prayer: "Lord, You've entrusted us with these girls. Now, since we're total amateurs, please help us to raise them as You would have us raise them."

I suppose it's inevitable that parts of this book will appear to some as Wolgemuth Home Movies. "Aw, come on, please . . . just *one* more slide tray from our summer at the Grand Canyon?"

Frankly, I'm embarrassed at the thought. What we have is a gift from God, including the girls and our relationships with them. Much of what we've learned has come from our experience of failure. In other words, if it sounds as though I have some things figured out, it's only because I made enough mistakes to know what doesn't work! I'm not showing off. You'll just have to believe me.

About This Book

Bobbie and I were thrust into this parenting thing pretty quickly. In many ways, we were just children ourselves. Bobbie was 21 when Missy was born, and I was 23. And now that the girls are older than we were when they were born, we've decided to document the process we went through in raising them.

Although many of the stories and illustrations refer to me in the singular, I assure you this job of raising girls has been a partnership.

Not only has my wife been an essential ally in the process, but she has also been a reservoir of sound information and advice.

Instead of tracing our experiences and the lessons we've learned in chronological order, I'll take you through seven major themes: Protection, conversation, affection, discipline, laughter, faith, and conduct.

Because I'm a hopeless tinkerer—a weekend warrior—the theme of "building" runs through the whole book. When I'm in the middle of a project and have to run to the store for more supplies, I grab a piece of scrap wood and make a list using the pencil that's usually tucked above my right ear. I do this because if I don't write it down, I'll forget. Don't laugh at me. You forget, too.

Anyway, at the end of chapters 2 through 10—the seven "principles" chapters and the last chapter—I've summarized the material in a "Builder's Checklist" so you can more easily access the information—also, so you won't forget.

You'll find many things in this book helpful for raising sons, too, but I've especially aimed these chapters at dads and daughters. According to some of my friends who have sons, there really is a difference, and, after all, raising girls is what I've been through.

Even though my fathering situation has been a traditional one, this book closes with an afterword that addresses the unique needs and concerns of dads in "special" situations. Thanks to friends who are divorced, single, or blended-family dads, I've been helped to understand some important differences in these environments.

You'll probably disagree with some of what you'll read. That's to be expected, and of course that's okay. If, however, in your disagreement, this book raises some good questions and you make progress toward your own effective parenting, then so much the better.

After you read this book, if you decide to give it to someone else to read—or you could go out and buy another copy—give it to a dad with a young daughter. The earlier a dad starts thinking through these principles, the better his chances will be of succeeding. Yet I think they'll prove helpful to any dad regardless of his daughter's age.

My prayer is that God will give you wisdom as you take on this huge and wonderful task of building a girl. Not just any girl, mind you, but *your* girl.

PART ONE

Someone who calls you

"Daddy"

What's a nice guy like you doing in a book like this?

"If I sat here for three or four weeks, I could not adequately describe just how important the father-daughter relationship is."

DR. JAMES DOBSON

"**A**re you awake?"

It had been almost an hour since we had gone to bed, but I knew my wife hadn't dozed off either, so I broke the silence with the question.

"Uh huh," came her quiet reply.

Then, trying not to sound too worried, I asked if she thought it was about time for us to hear our 15-year-old daughter walking through the front door. "When did Missy say she would be home?" I asked, mustering all the confidence I could to keep my voice from quivering.

"Around 11:00," returned my wife, her voice sounding strong and sure. She had decided to put on the same act.

We lay there for a few more minutes, neither of us speaking. Before asking the question, I had checked my nightstand clock. It was 11:25. I knew Missy was late—not a normal thing for her. More silence.

"Maybe we ought to make a call to see if we can find her," I finally said, losing most of my on-top-of-it tone of voice.

In a flash, Bobbie's nightstand lamp was on, and she was dialing. A sleepy youth pastor's wife finally picked up the phone. "Susan, this is Bobbie Wolgemuth, and I'm sorry to call you so late, but have Missy and David left your house?"

Although I couldn't hear Susan's answer, I could tell by Bobbie's tone as the conversation continued that the kids had left a long time before, with plenty of time to be home by now.

"Where's Missy?" Bobbie said as she hung up the phone, making no attempt to hide her frustration and fear.

Our daughter and her friend David had been at Mark and Susan's for a Sunday night Bible study. David was a 17-year-old boy who was like a brother to Missy and a son to us. A welcome "member" of our family, David would come and go from our house without ever knocking on the door. Our refrigerator was his refrigerator. We liked that.

But tonight, David was keeping me from going to sleep, and I wanted to know why.

We waited. Eleven forty-five, no Missy. Midnight, no Missy. Ten after twelve . . .

"I'm getting up," I finally announced. "I'm going downstairs to wait."

Bobbie said nothing. She was either praying for Missy or planning David's public execution down by the mall.

By the time I made it to the front door, David's car was turning into our driveway, his headlights sweeping across our house. "Finally," I said loud enough for Bobbie to hear me upstairs. "She's home."

Instead of trudging back up the stairs to bed, I thought I'd wait for Missy to get inside and explain where she had been and why she hadn't called.

David's car came to a stop, the headlights went out, the engine went quiet, and both David and Missy came bounding up the walk to the front door.

Standing there in nothing but my snow-white Jockey shorts, I quickly came to two realizations: (1) There was no time to dash up the stairs without being seen, and (2) if I stepped around the corner into the living room, no one would ever see me in that condition. In the next room, I found a good, shadowed spot.

The front door opened, and Missy came in with David right on her heels. *What's going on?* I wondered. *Don't these kids know what time it is?*

Missy scrambled up the stairs to get something, leaving David standing just inside the front door. For what seemed like a minute or two, he stood there, not having any idea that Missy's dad was just around the corner.

Then it happened. David began to move, and as he did, he started quietly humming. I could tell by the growing sound of the "music" that he was coming toward the living room.

I panicked, my mind dropping into overdrive. *If I tuck myself into the shadow next to the piano, he'll never see me.* I was proud of myself for thinking so quickly at that time of the night.

David walked to the doorway into the living room and stopped. Continuing to hum, he scanned the darkness. I felt like a fugitive, hiding from the long arm of the law . . . in my own house.

Unfortunately, David began to move again, coming right toward the piano where I was standing.

By the time he finally saw me, this unsuspecting, red-headed, 17-year-old boy was about 10 inches away. There he stood, Mr. All-Conference-Student-Leader-and-Everyone's-Favorite-Teenage-Boy. And there I stood, Tarzan of the Living Room.

"Hello, David," I said casually, as though I had bumped into him at a school function. "What are you doing here?"

The boy gasped, quickly sucking in just enough air to keep from collapsing in cardiac arrest. His body froze, but in the darkness, I could see his eyes moving up and down, scanning my terrific outfit.

At that moment, Missy burst into the living room. A stuffed animal the kids at church passed around like a mascot was tucked under her arm.

"Dad," she exclaimed, "what are *you* doing here?"

Good question.

What Are You Doing Here?

Whatever the reason you have this book in your hand, the fact is that you *are* here. Maybe you're a brand-new father of a baby girl and you want to find out what you're in for. Or perhaps your daughter has been around for a few years, and although you think you're doing a pretty good job as the daddy, you'd like some help. It could be that your daughter is just about to step across the threshold into womanhood, and you're a little nervous.

> *Being the father of a girl can be a journey into the great unknown, and there's no sense going it alone.*

Whatever the reason, I'm glad you're here. Being the father of a girl can be a journey into the great unknown, and there's no sense going it alone. You've spent your whole life as a male, so you know that if this were a son, you could give him a pointer or two from your own experience as he moves through his growing-up years. But this is a girl, and there are two things you know for sure: (1) She's your responsibility, and (2) you have no personal experience that will help you.

Artist's Rendering of the Finished Project

During my years in sales, I visited many corporate lobbies. While waiting for my appointment, I rarely sat down. Sitting makes me even more nervous than I would otherwise be. This was usually a source of frustration for the receptionist, who would repeatedly "order" me to sit by gently "inviting" me to take a seat.

Often as I'd walk around those impeccably decorated waiting areas, I would see on the wall a framed and colorful illustration—an artist's rendering—of the corporation's next building expansion.

Sometimes it was a new wing on the existing building, and sometimes it was a whole new building. In either case, given my love for construction, I would always be fascinated with those glimpses into the future, studying every detail.

Let's say that once the corporation found enough capital to proceed and all the bids were in, Cousin Larry's Construction Company got the project. If Cousin Larry was as smart as everyone said he was, he would have asked for that drawing to be hung in a place where his employees and subcontractors could see it every day. It would have been a great help to Larry and his people if they could begin—and continue—working on this project, focusing not on the necessary activities and details of any complex construction assignment, but on the *finished* product—the beautiful results.

In a similar way, the greatest challenge you'll face as the father of a daughter is to keep from being distracted by the day-to-day stuff— the little duties and challenges that can easily capture a dad's full-time attention. Instead, do what Cousin Larry did. Keep a "picture" in your mind of what it is you're building here: a healthy, poised, confident, balanced, and happy woman . . . a complete daughter who will someday be counted among your closest friends. Begin— and continue—building with the end in mind.

This book will help you do just that.

THE PROJECT OF A LIFETIME

Don't you love Saturday mornings? You go to bed late Friday night, knowing you can sleep in as long as you want because the weekend has arrived. But suppose one particular Saturday morning, something's wrong. You're lying in bed wide awake, and there's no going back to sleep.

The dawning sun is barely squeezing through the blinds. You

glance at the digital clock on your nightstand: 6:11! *So why is it so tough to wake up on a weekday when I have to get up,* you think, *but now that I can sleep as late as I want to, I'm lying here wide awake?*

The answer is simple. You've got a project. You've been looking forward to starting it for a long time. It's going to take a stack of pressure-treated wood, which was delivered this week.

You've been to The Home Depot (or whatever the huge, buy-every-possible-building-supply-you-could-ever-need-under-one-roof warehouse store is called where you live) and loaded up. "*Beep.* Someone in Plumbing dial 344." The guy in building supplies with the orange canvas bib that says "Hello, my name is Dave. Can I help you?" was actually quite helpful. Now you've got your galvanized nails and bolts, a new drill bit, and several bags of premixed concrete.

You can hardly wait to get started.

Because your wife *doesn't* have a project this morning, you quietly pull on a pair of old jeans and slip out your bedroom door, down the stairs, and into the garage where everything is waiting.

You and your wife have been talking about building a deck on the back of the house for a long time. You've walked around your backyard many times, surveying the site. You've even stood where the deck will be, envisioning your new view when it's done. And you have one of those propane gas grills on layaway, waiting for its new home.

Your neighbors have heard all about this deck, and frankly, they're hoping it looks great so they can (have you help them) build one, too.

This Little Girl of Ours

Because you're reading this book, you've probably stood at your wife's hospital bedside and looked into the squinting, ruddy face of a brand-new baby girl. Not, of course, just any baby girl, but *your* baby girl.

You know the awe, the thrill of realizing she's yours.

In fact, go back to that moment right now. What year was it? What was the name of the hospital? Do you remember your wife's doctor's name? What time of the year was it? What time of the day? How long had your wife been in labor? Were you tired? Was your wife tired? (I'm kidding.)

> *This is going to be the most unbelievable project you've ever tackled.*

Okay, are you standing there? It's an amazing moment—an absolutely breathtaking, speechless moment. You don't remember ever feeling such wonder.

Can you see yourself in that powder-blue hospital gown with those sterile "booties" stretched over your shoes, thinking, *Is this really happening to me? Is this little person actually mine? When am I going to be able to take her home? What will I do with her when I get her home? She looks so fragile. If I pick her up, will she break?*

What I want you to do is to see yourself looking at that baby, just as you stood in your backyard imagining the deck you were about to build. This is going to be the most unbelievable project you've ever tackled. You're responsible to help "build" this little girl into a woman. Sure, there are others who *could* do it, but you're the dad, and no one is more qualified than you.

And just like that Saturday morning when you couldn't sleep in, I want you to get excited about this project—very excited. In fact, I'll make you a promise: This project will give you more satisfaction than any deck possibly could.

And What About Tomorrow?

Now we're going on another journey. This one's into the future.

Your "little" girl has never looked more angelic than she does at this moment. The radiance of her face almost seems to be throwing off light. Her dress is the purest white you think you've ever seen.

The two of you are standing in front of closed double doors, and she has her arm gently tucked into yours. The organist begins playing, the doors open, and you and your daughter are slowly walking down the center aisle of a familiar place, your home church. You can feel your heart pounding in your temples. The people are standing. You look left and right into the faces of people you know. Extended family. Lifetime friends. You have never been more proud. You're having one of those out-of-body experiences where you can almost watch yourself. It's an overwhelming and awesome experience.

The walk to the front of the sanctuary has ended. You stand silently while the organist finishes the processional.

Except for a tingling sensation on the bottom of your feet, your whole body is numb, almost trancelike. You've been a guest at so many of these things and seen other dads standing with the bride, but you never expected it to be quite like this.

The minister has finished his opening remarks. You know he's getting close to asking you the big question. You're just about to place your girl into someone else's care for the rest of her life. For a split second, you panic.

What's my line? What's my cue? What am I supposed to say? Can someone please help me? Your mind screams for the words.

But just as you practiced the night before, when the minister asks you, "Who gives this woman to be married to this man," you speak the words that close the deal: "Her mother and I do."

You gently take her hand from your arm, place it into the minister's hand, and quietly sit down.

Several months ago, we attended a very formal wedding. Brittany, one of our daughter's best friends, was getting married. The church was impeccably decorated and packed from aisle to aisle with well-dressed guests. The strains of the organ swelled as the bride and her father walked to the front of the church. Everyone stood. It was one of those lump-in-your-throat moments.

As the majestic processional ended, the robed and somber minister opened a small, black book and read a few appropriate and, of course, formal remarks. His booming voice filled the sanctuary.

When he was finished, he invited the congregation to be seated. We obeyed.

Then, suddenly and without warning, the minister broke character. It was almost as though he had wakened from a spell. This big-city-seminary-trained and austere man of the cloth looked up from his little book and straight into the face of the bride's father. "Well, Johnny," he said, "I guess this is the end of the road."

Some of the guests snickered. Some laughed out loud. Fathers with unmarried daughters, including myself, audibly gasped.

Well, my fathering friend, someday when you take your own daughter for the short walk down that aisle, it *will be* the end of the road for you, too.

For some dads, helping their daughters pack all their grown-up things into a U-Haul and watching them drive off to seek their fortune will be that "walk down the aisle." In either case, they're setting their daughters free. What they've done to prepare them for that moment is finished.

This book will help you get ready for that moment.

You're What?

I fell into this fathering thing unexpectedly.

It was February 1971, just 11 months after our wedding. We were driving to Minneapolis from our home in Chicago to attend a business convention. I was glad Bobbie was able to come with me on this trip, but she seemed unusually tired as our car headed north into the bitter-cold night.

As I battled high winds and slippery highways, she spent most of the trip stretched out on the backseat, only occasionally waking to make sure I was okay. I scanned the radio dial, unsuccessfully trying to find something more interesting than hog futures.

I listened to Bobbie's irregular breathing from the backseat. I could tell this was more than just being extra tired. Bobbie wasn't feeling well.

I sure hope it's not the flu, I thought.

The day after we arrived in the Twin Cities, still not feeling right, she whispered her own diagnosis to me. Too overwhelmed to hear herself say the words above a whisper, she said softly, "Honey, I think I'm pregnant."

The words took my breath away. I couldn't believe it.

I was on the staff of a youth ministry, and she was a full-time college student. Because we lived on donations, our money lasted only a month at a time.

"What are we going to do?" she asked repeatedly during the next few days. The swirling reality of this responsibility began to sink in.

What *were* we going to do?

After our return to Chicago, Bobbie made an appointment with her doctor. She wanted to be sure. I went along for support.

The only man sitting in the waiting room, I remember scanning the women seated in the chairs around the perimeter of the room. They were at varying stages of readiness. Most were chatting openly with their neighbors about intimate and graphic details of physiological changes and surprises. I could feel the blood draining from my face. It was all I could do to hang on.

And then I saw her. My wife of less than one year walked from the examining room into the waiting room where I sat. Our eyes locked immediately. Hers welled up with tears. She nodded ever so slightly. She reminded me of an angel.

Pregnant on Purpose!

Most of our friends were married couples three or four years older than us. All of them had determined they were going to wait until they could "afford" children. And, I guess, without actually discussing it, that's where we were headed, too.

We suspected that these friends, once they learned we were expecting a baby, would be shocked. "You're pregnant? What happened? Surely this must be a big surprise!"

So, before any of those comments came our way, Bobbie and I sat down to talk it over.

"You know," I remember saying, "even though this really is a total shock, let's tell everyone this pregnancy was planned. We can't imagine how things are going to work out, but God has obviously blessed us with this baby, so, between you and me, let's just believe it was God's plan. Let's tell everyone that this baby was exactly what we had in mind."

Bobbie agreed, so that's what we decided to do.

And sure enough, friends asked. Some were subtle: "Hmm, what an interesting time in your lives to start a family." Others were really direct: "You're what?"

Even more surprising than the pregnancy itself to some of our friends was our confident response. I can still see them shaking their heads in pathetic disbelief.

The closer we got to delivery day, the more excited we became. The summer of 1971 was unusually warm and humid, even for Chicago. We bought a used air conditioning unit for the living room window, and Bobbie spent most of her last months of pregnancy standing directly in front of its coldest output.

In mid-September, our little girl was born.

What Did I Know About Girls?

I was disappointed. I'll admit it.

And though I didn't whisper a word of this to Bobbie, I really had wanted a boy—a son who would help me with building projects; a son I could tussle with on the living room floor; a son who, by some miraculous quirk of genetic fate, would be the athlete I never was. But it wasn't to be.

In three days, we brought our baby home from the hospital. And in no time, we discovered we were about to go through the adjustment of our lives. That adjustment made the passage from being single to getting married look like a walk in the park.

But there was no turning back. Try as we might to return to full nights of sleep and lazy, selfishly designed evenings, they were gone *forever.*

Who Are You, Little Girl? What's to Become of You?

Soon after Missy came home to live with us, I forgot the nonsense about the boy. This little person was capturing my heart. I couldn't wait to get home from work to look at her and hold her.

Late one afternoon, I was lying on the carpeted floor of our living room, cuddled next to her. She was on her tummy, a clean cloth diaper under her head, with her face turned toward me. I studied her tiny features—her velvety skin, little turned-up nose, and rosebud mouth.

We talked.

"Do you know who you are, little girl?" I asked. "You're Missy, and I'm your daddy. Do you know how glad I am that you came to live at our house? Do you know how much I love you?"

Occasionally her eyes would seem to focus.

I raised up enough to lean over and kiss her soft cheek. My hand rested on her back, softly patting. Drool trickled out of the corner of her mouth.

As though it were yesterday, I can remember the breathtaking feeling in my soul, not unlike the moment a roller coaster begins its descent.

"This little girl is my responsibility," I breathed out loud. "I'm her daddy, the only one she'll ever have."

The feeling was overwhelming, but not a frustrated or fearful kind of overwhelmed. I felt resolved. Committed. Ready to tackle the obstacles that would surely lie ahead.

I remember thinking, lying there next to this baby person, *I'll be your daddy, little girl. You can count on me. I can do this. I know I can. God, please help me.*

My project had begun.

CHAPTER TWO

Hanging in there: *Sure, I can finish this today*

"That which we persist in doing becomes easier—not that the nature of the task has changed, but our ability to do has increased."

RALPH WALDO EMERSON

It's a lot easier for me to start a project than to finish one. Why? Because I am, at the core of my being, a quitter. Although I suspected this about myself during my growing-up years, it came into clear focus during the summer of 1968.

Without really thinking it through, along with 39 friends who apparently didn't think it through either, I ventured out on a bicycle trip from San Francisco. We were headed for New York City. Between those two cities, I was ready to quit many times, and only the peer pressure of the group kept me from doing just that.

Our first day on the road started like some kind of party. The press were there taking photos of our group, with the Golden Gate Bridge providing a spectacular backdrop. As our police motorcycle escort whisked us through the cities of San Francisco and Oakland, we college men felt like Olympic marathoners, entering the stadium for the final two laps. Crowds gathered on the sidewalks—children waved and cheered, dogs barked, men stood at attention with their hands over their hearts, and women softly cried. (All this is true except for the part about the men and women.)

Unfortunately, unlike the marathoners at the end of their run, our trip was just beginning. We had 4,000 miles to go!

On our way to Walnut Creek, directly out of Oakland, we headed north on St. Mary's Road—the county tricked us into using this road by giving it a gentle, pious-sounding name. In only a few miles, we went from sea level to an altitude of almost 2,000 feet. I thought I was going to die. My greatest disappointment was that I didn't.

Riding one of the first versions of a 10-speed bike, I had, before this day, spent little time in first gear. The few times I had tried it, it seemed as if my feet were traveling faster than the wheels were turning. It was so easy to pedal, I almost fell off the bike.

But this particular afternoon—the whole afternoon—was spent in first gear. I kept checking to see if my tires were flat. *This must be what it's like to jog in waist-deep molasses,* I thought. My legs ached, and my chest felt as though it were about to burst into flames.

I decided that starting this trek had been great fun, but I really didn't want to finish it. Realizing I had 41 more days to go and that I had made the mistake of a lifetime, I decided to cash it in. If I had found someone to swap with, I would have traded my bike for a one-way bus ticket home in a second. No question about it. Unfortunately, I found no one to make the trade.

Forty-two days later, I stood on the easternmost banks of New York Harbor, staring at Lady Liberty. For every single day of the previous six weeks, I had peddled a 28-pound Schwinn Super Sport from dawn to dusk. No days off. No relief for my aching legs or terminally bruised rear end. No sleeping in a bed or eating my mother's cooking.

But, amazingly, this quitter had made it.

There was the day of riding on Highway 160, between Cortez and Durango, Colorado, suffering from the worst case of diarrhea I had ever experienced. In spite of having been on the road for almost two weeks, I lost six *more* pounds that day. My stomach ached so badly that I spent most of the day crying. I wanted desperately to quit. But I didn't.

And when I didn't, I thought, *Hey, I didn't quit. I wanted to quit. I schemed of how I could talk my way out of being too embarrassed by quitting, but I didn't do it. I didn't quit.*

In Missouri, Kenny Parks thought he'd tighten the quick-release hub on his front wheel with his foot, but instead he stuck his tennis shoe directly into the spokes. Unfortunately, I was riding about 10 inches behind him, and in a moment we were both tumbling down the asphalt—bicycle, Kenny, bicycle, me, bicycle, Kenny, bicycle, me, etc.

When the tumbling finished, I lay there on Highway 65, just west of Marshall, and wanted to quit again. The palms of my hands were skinned and bleeding. My legs were cut and scraped. I had had enough of this trip. I wanted to quit, but I didn't.

And when I didn't, I thought, *Hey, I didn't quit. I wanted to quit. My bleeding and bruised body wanted to quit, but I told it not to quit, and it obeyed.*

Two weeks later, a few miles east of Morristown, New Jersey, on Highway 24, it happened again. This time Kenny Parks was showing off and bounced his bike into a concrete curb. Instantly his wheel snapped into a twisted coil, and he was down. Because I had forgotten about Missouri, I was again just a few inches behind him. In a split second, we were both tumbling down the asphalt—bicycle, Kenny, bicycle, me, etc.

And even though we were only a hundred miles from the east coast, I wanted to quit. What I *had* done was fairly significant. After all, I had made it all the way to New Jersey. I wasn't completely finished, but I was *almost* finished. Close enough.

I had had enough of this bicycle trip—and Kenny Parks. I wanted to quit, but I didn't. And when I didn't, I thought, *Hey, I didn't quit. I wanted to quit, but I didn't. I may be a quitter by nature, but that doesn't mean I have to quit.*

The Peril of Underestimation

I'm not sure why, but in addition to being a quitter by nature, I'm a bad guesser—especially when it comes to estimating when I'm

going to be able to finish something. It can be anything—a trip to
the gas station, a call to a customer or client, or a building project.
Hundreds of times, I've heard myself promising Bobbie, "I'll be
finished today."

I've really meant it, too. I wasn't lying—at least, not intentionally.
Don't I get some credit for not "meaning" to lie?
I really thought I could finish something before
the sun went down, but in reality, it took me
many additional days—or weeks or months.

> *Things usually take longer than we had planned.*

I've learned I have a lot of company as a quitter. And maybe that's because things usually take
longer than we had planned—sometimes a lot longer. We get all
fired up in the beginning, but the fire fades. It's not the kick we
thought it was going to be. *This feels an awful lot like work.*

Please Read This Carefully

You may be wondering where I'm going with all this stuff, but please
stay with me. What follows may be the most important part of this
book.

When your daughter was born, you were euphoric. You thought,
I'm a daddy. Being a daddy is so much fun. You even told your
friends how much fun you were having.

But soon after your little girl came to live with you, your "legs"
began to ache, your "palms were bleeding and sore." You found
yourself wondering if you could take this one back. You turned your
girl over, hoping to see "Refundable" or "Return for Deposit" stamped
somewhere. No such luck.

This one was a keeper. There was no turning back.

Now I want you to admit something. In fact, I want you to say it
out loud. Yes, in spite of sounding like your mother, I want you to say

it out loud this minute. Don't mumble the words, but speak them forcefully. Ready? Here they are:

"I'd rather start a project than finish it."

Did you say that? Congratulations if you did.

If you didn't say those words out loud, go back and try again. Why did I ask you to do this? Because if you're like me—and you know who you are—you are a quitter. Rather than see a project through to completion, you'd prefer to start it and, when it stops being fun, walk away. I'm talking about totally completing something—all-the-scraps-of-wood-and-stuff-tossed-in-the-trash-and-tools-put-away completed.

But now that you've got this little girl living in your house, it's your job to help "build" her. You can't quit.

When she cries in the night—all night—for the fifth night in a row, you can't quit. When she rides her tricycle too close to your car and lays down a razor-fine scrape from front to back, you can't quit. When you try every bribe in the book to get her to pick up after herself and she just can't seem to do it, you can't quit. When her grades drop because she's having so much fun, you can't quit.

What's worse, building this girl is a project that's going to take a long, long time. In most cases, it will take about 20 years to finish. Your mileage may vary, depending on conditions. But don't quit. Don't let her get potty trained, then let her go. Don't let her get to grade-school age, then let her go. Don't let her get to her teenage years, then let her go. Don't let yourself think, *Well, I've done pretty well so far. After all, I did make it all the way to New Jersey.*

Building this girl is your job, it's going to take longer than you think, and you've got to make it the whole way to the end.

A Free Agent

Having said all this about not quitting, I need to remind you that your girl is a free agent. Nothing you can do will ever force her into a certain kind of thinking or behavior. Like it or not, there are no guarantees. There are no risk-free formulas. You're dealing with a person who has her own agenda, her own mind and will. Ultimately, she'll think and do what she decides to think and do.

> *You're dealing with a person who has her own agenda, her own mind and will.*

However, and this is a big *however,* you *can* create an environment that gives you—and her—the best shot at success. There are certain things you can do that will raise your probability of success.

That's what this book is about—low-risk fathering.

Step Right Up

I've never been a successful gambler. Who knows, maybe if I had experienced some success early in life, I would have wound up in a Las Vegas gutter, homeless and broke. The few times I tried my hand at gambling—or even simple betting—I got burned in a major way.

As a kid, I could single-handedly break my favorite major league baseball team's winning streak by betting they'd win one more game. If you're also a Cubs fan, I'm sorry to have been the sole reason for their perennial failure.

In college, I launched a chain-letter kind of get-rich-quick scheme using United States Savings Bonds. Just as it was really getting off the ground, Sam Delcamp, our dean, told me to shut it down or I'd be expelled from school. That night, I went door to door in every men's dormitory, asking that the chain letter be stopped. I also asked each man how much money he would personally lose by stopping the letter immediately. I promised to pay the money back to every one of them, which cost me all my wages from the next summer's construction work.

For some reason, regular, garden-variety gambling has been very, very bad to me.

With all undue respect to the world of wagers and bets, fathering your daughter is a gamble. It's about odds-making and long shots. It's about rolling the dice and holding your breath. It's about doing your best, then hoping, believing, and praying—especially praying.

In his best-selling book *Parenting Isn't for Cowards,* Dr. James Dobson talks to parents who, despite doing everything "right," have children who turn out "wrong." Naturally they feel guilty about it.

He remembers an outdoor wedding he and his wife attended where, the moment the bridegroom kissed his new bride, many brilliantly colored, helium-filled balloons were released.

At first the balloons seemed to hang together. But soon the slight breeze, combined with the varying amounts of helium in each balloon, had them separated, some by vast amounts of space.

Most of those brightly colored delights soared higher and higher. A few, however, seemed to have difficulty. Instead of sailing upward, they hovered near the treetops. Some even brushed along high-tension electrical wires, exploding with a loud pop.

Isn't it interesting that all those balloons, filled with the same kind of helium and released at the same moment, could have such diverse ends?

Of course, his point was to be an encouragement to parents whose children were the hovering kind rather than the soaring kind—especially those parents with more than one child and with different results in each. The same parents, with basically the same external influences, could get greatly diverse outcomes.

So did Dr. Dobson mean you should just spontaneously throw yourself at this job of building your daughter with no plan, hoping for the best, believing that what will be, will be?

No, absolutely not! Don't ever do anything so foolish.

Safety First

I used to think football players lifted weights and ran wind sprints so they could win. But actually, winning is the second-most-important reason they endure all that training pain.

During the early spring of 1994, I had the opportunity to walk through the new North Dallas training facility of the Cowboys with safety Bill Bates. Bill has the reputation of being one of the toughest men to ever play professional football. I asked him about working out and why he did it four to six hours per day year 'round.

I was surprised to hear that the primary reason football players put themselves through the pain of daily workouts is to *protect* themselves from being seriously hurt on the field. The only reason more players aren't literally killed in action is that they're in great shape. How else could they walk away from some of those incredible collisions?

They build their muscles to lower—although, unfortunately, not to eliminate—the risk of serious injury. It's gambling with the odds in their favor.

When I use one of my power saws, I always wear goggles. Why? Well, in addition to making me look cool to the neighbors ("Wow, Robert must be doing something dangerous. See, he's wearing protective eye wear!"), they lower the risk of eye injury. Do they totally eliminate the risk? No. I suppose that even though they're made with space-age plastic, something *could* fly up and shatter them in my face. I wear them because working with power equipment is a gamble. My bet is that I won't get hurt. The goggles improve my chances of being right.

You're a dad. You've got a daughter, and raising her to be a happy and well-balanced woman is a gamble. As she grows, without doing this intentionally, her "bet" is that she's going to turn out to be a self-willed, incorrigible rebel, an embarrassment to you and her mother. Her natural tug will commonly be toward getting herself off the track on her journey toward "completeness." Your "bet" is that she's going to stay on that track and make you proud. Doing what this book suggests won't guarantee that you'll win. However, I promise that doing what this book suggests will increase your odds of success.

So consider the next seven chapters to be free weights and treadmills; laps around the track and stair machines; fathering goggles, if you will.

My hope is that you'll not only make it through, but that you'll also enjoy *victory*—the safe completion of a beautiful redwood deck, as it were, and lots of delicious hamburgers on that gas grill.

And don't forget to finish. Go all the way to the very end. You can do it.

BUILDER'S CHECKLIST

1. It's a lot easier to start projects than it is to finish them. But when you do push ahead, resisting the temptation to quit, you discover a payoff that's well worth the sacrifice.

2. Now that your daughter is home, she's a keeper. You can't take her back for a refund.

3. Professional football players get in shape to reduce their odds of injury. Doing the right thing with your daughter won't guarantee success, but it will increase your chances.

4. Someone has joked that he finds himself praying, "Lord, give me patience . . . and give it to me now!" Of course, praying for patience is no laughing matter. Take some time—right now seems like a good opportunity—and pray for patience with your daughter. If you need help, pray the following:

Lord, I am a quitter. It's much easier for me to start than to finish. And, there are times when I get very impatient with _____. Sometimes I feel like a failure, and I want to quit. Lord, I confess that I need You to help me persevere. Please help me to be a loving, gracious, enduring, and patient dad. Amen.

PART TWO

Never too tough, never too tender

Seven things you must know

Protection:

Able to leap tall buildings in a single bound

"It is difficult to give children a sense of security unless you have it yourself. If you have it, they catch it from you."

DR. WILLIAM C. MENNINGER

I made the decision to do "something" about dating way back when our second daughter, Julie, was in sixth grade. She had, unbeknownst to us, agreed to "go with" another sixth-grader named Vincent. Two months after this romance had begun, Vincent called our house. Missy, Julie's older sister, answered the phone. After identifying himself, Vincent asked Missy if Julie was home. She wasn't. So Vincent asked Missy to give Julie the following message: "Tell her she's dumped."

I decided we could do better than that.

Four years later, Julie turned 16. Coming home from work one evening, as I wheeled my car into our driveway, the two-door European sedan parked in front of our house caught my eye. "Nice," I remember whispering out loud. "Very nice."

Steven was a senior. I had already suspected he was interested in Julie because of his recent visits to our church and Sunday school. Julie was only a week short of her sixteenth birthday, and Steven knew the rules: no "single" dating until Julie had turned 16, and boys must be "interviewed" by me.

I walked through the kitchen into the family room, where Bobbie, Julie, and Steven were sitting, making small talk.

Steven quickly stood. "Good evening, Mr. Wolgemuth," he said, squeezing out a thin, nervous smile.

"Hi, Steven. How are you?" I replied, firmly shaking his hand.

"Fine." His lips were white.

Following a few seconds of silence, I spoke again. "How about if we go into the next room for a few minutes?"

His visit to our house was to get this meeting out of the way. He knew it was part of the deal, and he was ready.

Steven was tall and handsome, with steel-blue eyes, curly, blond hair, and a winsome smile. He was a varsity basketball player with a physique to match. He followed me into my study, where I invited him to sit in the chair across from my desk.

Again, after just a moment of silence, I broke in. "I couldn't help but notice the car out front when I drove in," I said. "Is it yours?"

"Yes, sir," Steven replied, displaying his best manners. "My dad is helping with the payments, but I cover the insurance and gas. We bought it last summer, and I spent a lot of time fixing it up. The engine was in pretty good shape, but the body needed some work."

That was a lot more information than I was looking for, but I let him run. He was taking the bait. After a few more minutes of detail about what he had done to the car, I leaned back in my chair.

"It sounds like this is a pretty special car," I said, leading him deeper. He nodded as I continued: "Now, can I ask you a question?"

"Okay, go ahead," he replied.

"What if I had come to your house last night, knocked on the door, and asked if I could borrow your car for the evening? What would you have said?"

Steven took no time to respond: "I'd have said 'No way.'"

Poor kid, I thought. *You've had it now.*

"Why?" I replied, acting as though his answer fascinated me.

"Well, because I don't know you. I don't know how you drive. I don't know how you'd treat my car. I'm not sure I can trust you. That car's important to me." Steven's narrowed eyes let me know he was very serious.

When he finished, I leaned forward on my elbows, taking just a moment to make sure he was listening carefully. "That's interesting, Steven," I finally said. "I know exactly what you're saying. If I were you, I'd do the same thing."

He smiled and, for the first time, looked a little relaxed. Some color was returning to his lips. "You would?" he said.

"Absolutely," I reassured him. "And do you want to know why?" I gave him no time to answer. "Because tonight you've come to my house and asked if you can *borrow* our daughter for the evening. And before I let you do that, I want to find out who you are."

A shocked but dawning look of understanding crossed his face— an interesting mix of discovery and nausea. I had his undivided attention. I double-checked to be sure he was still breathing.

Believe it or not, the conversation that followed wasn't adversarial. I actually found myself liking Steven. All things considered, he seemed like a nice young man. As we talked, I reminded him that, as an 18-year-old, he was far more experienced than Julie. I expected him to treat her the way he treated his four-wheeled import. No, actually, better.

He understood.

We talked about what was important to him—his sports, his family, his favorite subjects in school, his plans for next year, and his faith. I told him a little about our family and assured him he would always be welcome in our home. I told him our daughter's friends were our friends. He seemed appreciative.

When we finished our conversation, we both stood up. I shook his hand.

"You know, Mr. Wolgemuth," he said, "if I ever have a 16-year-old daughter of my own, I'll do what you did today."

"Thank you, Steven," I replied. "It means a lot that you would say that."

I walked him to the family room, where Bobbie and Julie were waiting. They later told me they had been praying for him. "Good-bye, Steven," I said. "I'll see you around."

"Good-bye, Mr. Wolgemuth."

Protection From . . .

In one of our scrapbooks is a picture that Bobbie took of me in 1971, lying on my stomach across our bed. I'm sleeping, and my arms are above my head in a curved position, like the right-turn signal you learned in bicycle safety. Sleeping inside the space made by my arm and my head is this miniature person. Missy's head is no bigger than my palm. Her little clenched hands are the size of walnuts.

> *The nature of your protection changes as your daughter grows.*

In the photo, she looks so fragile and absolutely breakable. And she was.

Your job as a dad is to protect your daughter. The nature of this protection, of course, changes as she grows, and it's your job to make the adjustments appropriately. When she's crawling toward a roaring fireplace, you yank her back. When her tricycle is heading for the street, you sprint down the driveway to stop it. And when you launch her into the hostile environment of growing up, you stand guard.

Why? Because she needs it. And, as we'll talk about later, she wants it.

The need for protection is evident when your girl is small. Nearly everything presents its own unique opportunity for potential danger.

"Be careful of the stove, Honey, the kettle is hot. Hot. Haaahhhttt!" You act as if you're touching the kettle yourself. You quickly pull your hand back. Your eyes get big. "Ooowwwweeee. See, Sweet-heart? Hot."

"Leave that doggie alone, Baby. Look at those big teeth! I think he's angry. He might bite you if you don't stop pulling his ear. Let's see if we can find something else to do."

Your job is to provide a safe haven. Whether it's from being attacked by a coiled snake lurking in your vegetable garden or from the longing eyes of an 18-year-old athlete, your job is to protect.

I've Got Everything Under Control . . . Almost

I learned an important lesson about the need to keep an eye on small children the hard way. On an award-winning, spring Saturday morning, Bobbie told me she was going to spend several hours with a friend at a craft bazaar. My job was to watch the girls, who were four and a half and one and a half at the time.

I assured her I would have everything under control. *How hard can it be to baby-sit the girls for a few hours?* I figured.

Over the years, I've discovered that many dads think of an assign-ment like "Keep an eye on the kids" the same way they would regard a request to "Keep an eye on the smoke alarm." If it's not wailing at plaster-cracking decibels, it must be okay.

That Saturday morning, I was one of those dads.

I was in the garage, sharpening the blade on my lawn mower. The girls were in the front yard, playing duck-duck-goose with their friend Laura Green. Except for an occasional happy squeal, I heard nothing. All seemed well.

After a while, Missy came into the garage to retrieve the stroller. Their game had lost its charm, and she and Laura were going to take Julie for a little ride. "Be careful," I warned without even looking up. *Girls are so easy,* I thought.

Our stroller was an inexpensive and flimsy portable model that folded into something not much bigger than an umbrella. (This was before the government set standards that now require strollers to be substantial enough to tow a ski boat.) And for the next several minutes, Missy and Laura took turns pushing Julie back and forth on the sidewalk in front of our house.

Then, because little girls can get bored quickly, they decided to make up a new game. This game was called "Let's take the stroller to the top of our steep driveway and see how fast we can get it going on its own"—with Julie still on board, of course.

Oblivious to the girls' new game, I continued to file away. My lawn mower blade was looking good. *This thing will take out small trees*, I mused.

Missy stood at the top of the driveway. Laura waited at the bottom to keep Julie and the stroller from flying into the street. They were all having a big time. But apparently, after a few breakneck voyages to the sidewalk, Julie decided to get creative. *I wonder what would happen if I took my feet off this little footrest and tried to stop this thing myself,* she must have thought, because the next time down, she jammed her little sneakers down onto the asphalt.

The physics of the speeding stroller wouldn't allow for tiny, screeching shoes to bring it to a safe stop. Instead, the stroller flipped forward, end over end, until it came to rest at the bottom of the driveway.

The smoke alarm began to wail—no, actually, two alarms, Julie and Missy.

By the time I reached the girls, they were both out of control. Laura had already made plane reservations for South America and was on her way to the airport.

Julie, still partially in the stroller, was lying on her side, her nose and lips bleeding. I knelt next to her, a sense of panic sweeping over me. *I wonder if she'll heal up before Bobbie gets back?* I remember thinking. I tried to comfort Julie, reassuring her she was all right. Suddenly I thought, *I wonder what this did to her teeth?*

Gently opening her mouth, I was met with a horrible sight. The full force of the initial impact must have centered on Julie's teeth, slamming them into the driveway. The black tar from the asphalt covered both her front teeth. With all the blood, I had no idea if they were chipped or, worse, completely broken off.

I'm a dead man, raced through my mind. *How will I ever explain this to Bobbie?*

The truth is, I had failed. My job had been to watch the girls, and I hadn't.

When Bobbie got home, she let me have it. I asked if she'd like to see how sharp my lawn mower blade was, but she didn't seem interested.

Gratefully, Julie's baby teeth were only slightly chipped, and the swollen lips healed nicely. But that spring day, I learned a vital lesson: Protecting my daughter can never be a careless afterthought.

Physical Versus Emotional Protection

If there's one word to describe your baby when you bring her home from the hospital, it's *helpless.* This baby can do absolutely nothing for herself. She would literally perish without constant care. Her needs are for physical protection.

From that moment on, however, her physical helplessness will diminish a day at a time. Each new step in her development will announce one more place where she can do things herself. From holding her head up on the changing table and tying her own shoes all the way to finding her way through big-city traffic, she'll need your physical protection less and less.

Jay Kesler tells the story of the mother wren. As her chicks' fuzzy down begins turning into real feathers, the mother decides it's time for flying lessons. Because this wise parent understands the value of diminishing physical protection, she takes her babies on a short journey, a field trip just a few feet down the branch, then safely back to the nest.

Several days later, the journey may take the awkward little birds a bit farther down the branch—but always under the mother's watchful eye.

Eventually, the mother wren, determining her brood is ready for the challenges of the neighbor cat, kicks them out of the nest to fly on their own. Interestingly, the wrens with their newfound freedom still return to the nest for several days. Soon, however, they're gone forever to live in a sorority house with dozens of other birds. Father Wren agrees to pay the tuition for many years to come.

This is exactly as it should be—progressive physical independence. Your daughter is taught, she experiences the growth and development, then she actually exercises those new and independent characteristics and skills.

Two Examples

When she begins to crawl, you're going to have to child-proof your house. Anything she can crawl to and open, break, or pull down on herself has to be removed.

When Missy and Julie were this age, we put safety catches on all the kitchen and bathroom cabinet doors. What a nuisance they were! But dish-washing detergent and toilet-bowl cleaner look mighty delicious when you're six months old.

Tall, thin end tables or plant stands are easily pulled down as your little girl learns the art of pulling herself up from her knees. And delicate glass figurines or sharp objects need to be moved to a high shelf. Don't worry, you'll be able to restore everything to its rightful place before you know it. Oh, you're going to have lots more kids? Maybe you ought to go ahead and have a garage sale or give some of this stuff away as gifts. (Isn't that where *you* got it?)

The dog's water and the cat's litter box are going to have to go somewhere. Don't ask me where; we didn't have pets until the girls were much older. We *tried* a puppy, but Missy kept putting its face in her mouth.

After those first steps, the plot thickens. In no time, you're going to wonder why you were so eager to see your little girl walk! The crawling trip from the living room to the kitchen, which used to take a few minutes, now seems almost instantaneous. She's here one moment and gone the next.

During the first few years of our older daughter's life, we had the luxury of living close to my parents. Sunday-after-church dinner was a regular ritual. We loved giving Missy a chance to get to know her grandparents.

One particular spring Sunday, my brother and his wife were there. Their daughter, Kristin, only three months older than Missy, had become our little girl's best friend. Conversation between a couple of two-year-old girls is pretty funny stuff.

Dinner was over, and the whole family was standing in the kitchen with my mother, drying the dishes. Someone looked out the window to see two little girls walking hand in hand only a few hundred feet from Roosevelt Road, the busiest four-lane west of Chicago.

A track star in high school, my mother was there in a moment, scooping up those two adventuring children. Bobbie and I never forgot the lesson: As soon as she can walk, she will! Keep an eye on her.

The Process of Physically Unprotecting

While she's still in your nest, hands-on protection comes in the form of physically taking your child away from danger. Your girl depends on you to make all her protective decisions. If she's close to danger, you yank her away from it. No discussion. No questions asked.

Soon, you demonstrate and teach about danger. Eventually, that gives way to allowing her to test what she's learned. You give her a "few feet" to hop from the nest, then back again—nothing involving life and death.

After years of watchful protection, you don't suddenly say to your child, "Well, I've been protecting you from all these dangerous things, but now it's time you learned how to fend for yourself. So your mother and I are going to go away for the weekend. Before we leave, we're going to turn on everything in the house that's electronic and potentially deadly, put all the cleansers and prescription drugs out where you can get to them, and then just set you loose in here. When we get back, if you've survived, we'll set your toy box on the street, where you can spend the next day."

No, as she grows, you "invite" her out of the nest a few feet at a time. You give her a chance to spread her wings just a little—a chance where, if she makes a mistake, she hasn't done any severe damage to herself or anyone else.

The process of going from physically protecting to unprotecting your girl is the systematic process of showing and teaching her what's dangerous and what's safe. Then, like the mother wren, you let her go on some "field trips" away from you.

Baby-sitters

Find money in your budget for baby-sitters. Of course, going out without your little one gives you and your wife some relief from the relentless demands of parenting. But leaving your girl with someone else also gives her a taste of independence—making decisions on her own regarding what's safe and what's not.

What she'll learn is that sharp things are sharp even if you and your wife are 10 miles away. Breakable things are still breakable even if you're not there to say your predictable "Be carefuls."

Occasionally I run into a set of parents who proudly announce that they haven't spent a night away from their two-year-old. Although I believe their motives—not wanting to expose their child to danger or the unpredictability of life without them—are admirable, they're forgetting the need to physically unprotect in a regular, systematic way, helping their child to make all of Mom's and Dad's verbal cautions their own from personal experience. *Hmm, Mom was right, jumping on the bed can lead to falling off the bed, and falling off the bed hurts. Wow, Dad was right, this knife is dangerous!*

Church

Have you noticed there are couples who, after they have their first baby, seem to disappear from church? They were so faithful, and now they're gone. So you call them and discover they're afraid the little one will be exposed to physical danger or germs. "We're going to keep the baby home for a few years," they say.

> *If God didn't think He could protect your baby in His own house, why would He have created nurseries?*

This is faulty thinking, because if God didn't think He could protect your baby in His own house, why would He have created nurseries?

Church is going to be a hop down the branch for your girl. She's going to learn that your admonition to "Be nice to other children" is for her own protection. You'll be sitting there in "big church," singing hymn number 396, and your daughter will either witness or personally experience—you hope it's witness—the pain of retaliation for the unauthorized "borrowing" of another child's toy. And she'll think, *Hmm, Dad was right. Sharing doesn't hurt as much as not sharing does!*

A successful field trip.

Grade school is another example of where other children come into play. Fellow students usually provide solid companionship for your daughter, and rarely do they present physical dangers. However, the need for your emotional protection begins to climb. If this were a book for sons, I'd suggest a course at your neighborhood YMCA on self-defense.

Emotional Protection

Your daughter's need for your emotional protection is far less visible or predictable than her need for physical protection. Its form may change from day to day, but it's just as important. Physical protection may seem more urgent when your girl is a tiny baby, especially if your family is healthy and loving. But as she grows and relates more and more with others, the need for your emotional protection also grows.

Soon after we brought our first girl home from the hospital, I developed an interest in gardening. No one was more surprised than me, since yard work had been nothing but drudgery from the time I had been able to push an unmotorized lawn mower. But my older brother had introduced me to roses. I bought a couple dozen prize-winners and was off and running.

One particular June weekend, I was behind the house, clipping, dusting, pruning, fertilizing, and spraying. Out of the corner of my eye, I noticed Missy, three and a half then, dashing through the yard for the back door. She opened it just wide enough for her face and called, "Mommy!"

"Yes, Missy," came the voice of her mother from the other end of the house.

"Are you there?"

"Of course, Missy," came the reply. "I'm here."

Closing the door, Missy ran around to the front of the house.

I continued to work on my roses, curious about what I had seen.

Several minutes later, Missy appeared again, running to the back door. Again she opened it just enough for her little face and called out, "Mommy!"

"Yes, Missy, what is it?"

"Are you there?"

"Yes, Honey, I'm here."

Again she closed the door and returned to the front of the house.

Curiosity got the best of me. Without being seen, I crept around to the front of the house to see what was going on.

Two of the older neighborhood girls had drawn a "hopscotch" court on the sidewalk with a piece of chalk. After playing several games alone, they apparently had invited Missy to join in. However, at three and a half, she hadn't been briefed on how to play the game. But instead of teaching her what to do, the older girls had left Missy to figure it out for herself. And, of course, she was doing it wrong—wrong square, wrong leg, wrong everything. This provided the girls a little comic relief at Missy's expense.

In her little spirit, she knew something was wrong. So once Missy had finished her turn, she laid her marker on the sidewalk and ran around to the back door. Somehow understanding that she was being laughed "at," she needed the emotional protection of her mother's voice. And, apparently, it was enough.

Protect, Don't Lecture

Dads are especially susceptible to turning an emotional-protecting opportunity into a veritable classroom, good enough for credit at the local junior college.

Bobbie and I have friends, Dave and Jan, whose daughter, Ashley, came running through the family room door one time when she was six years old. She was sobbing between deep gasps. When they had finally calmed her down enough for her to speak, she told them about the little girl across the street—how she had grabbed Ashley's finger painting from school (one more crinkly and brittle underwater seascape for the refrigerator door) and torn it in half.

"My first impulse," Dave later told me, "was to ask a few questions. Seize the moment. 'Why did your friend do such an ugly thing to you? What did *you* do to make her so unhappy? You *must* have done something to upset her.' Then I realized that my little girl needed no lecture. This was not a teaching opportunity for me."

Dave had put his newspaper down. He turned to his daughter and opened his arms. He held her until the crying had subsided. He didn't say a thing.

"What dawned on me, as my daughter's tears began soaking through my shirt," Dave told me, "was that life was about angry neighbor kids. About injustice. And about consequences. Ashley was crying, and whatever had happened, she was paying for it with her own tears. She needed safety. Protection. So I gave it to her. A stout lecture would have ruined this tender moment. The lesson had already been learned. There would be other times for lectures."

Whose Garden Is This?

In 1971, our company moved into a new office building. It was out in an area that someday would be completely developed with commercial buildings, but ours was the first building on a new street. Since there was a lot of open space around us, we asked the developer if we could parcel out some land among our employees for vegetable gardens.

He said that would be no problem. He warned us, however, that if the land should sell before harvest time, we'd have to understand. Tomato plants don't hold up well when confronted by a bulldozer's scoop.

So I planted a vegetable garden. It was great. I rented a Rototiller, got the dirt all nice and loose, and bought seeds. (If you do ever do this, buy squash. Zucchini squash will make you feel powerful as a gardener. Those leaves grow overnight and are huge.) Having my very own vegetable garden was so much fun.

Because this garden was a few hundred yards from any water sources, I had to water it by hand. And as it got into late June and early July, my plants didn't look as good as they had before. So one day I went out and had a little talk with my garden. I said to those plants, "You're a disgrace. Just look at you. I mean, you're getting all ugly and brown. Some of your lower leaves are falling off. Some of them are wilted. Some of them even look dead. You ought to be ashamed."

To be honest, that conversation didn't really happen. Actually, June was a little dry that year, and those leaves *did* get a little brown. But I decided that if I was going to enjoy any harvest, I would have to carry water. I let them die. That's why there's a produce department at our grocery store.

Sometimes a dad surveys his family and says, "Just look at you. You're misbehaved and out of control. Why don't you just shape up?"

Guess whose responsibility this protection and nurture thing is? Guess who's responsible, even on a "hot July day" after you've put in a full day of your own work, to "carry the water," even if you have to carry it in jugs a few hundred yards?

You *can* do it.

"How Did It Make You Feel When . . ."

There's a magic phrase that will unlock your girl's emotions and give you an opportunity to protect. I encourage you, even when she's just beginning to talk, to start lots of questions with it: "How did it make you feel when . . ."

After my friend Dave had held Ashley long enough for her tears to subside, his first question to her should have been, "How did it make you feel when the little girl tore your paper in half?" And, as Ashley was describing what "hurt feelings" looked like to her, Dave should have been listening carefully, occasionally saying things like "I understand" and "That must really make you sad."

In doing this, Dave would be giving Ashley permission to express her emotional pain. He would also be giving her a safe environment—a protected place—in which to express it. Professionals tell us that when emotional pain is locked in the subconscious mind, it often gets infected, creating a far more dangerous situation in later years. Your invitation to your girl to tell you how she's feeling will bring those emotions into the light of day, giving them a chance to heal.

Boys . . . a Reprise

When our girls turned 13, I took them out to dinner. I chose a place they would consider expensive. What was important was that *they* thought it was a big deal.

During the dinner, I explained to them that over the next few years, there would be other men in their lives. Young men would begin to notice them and, perhaps, take a certain liking to them.

Then I presented them with a gift. Missy got a key with a tiny diamond chip on the top, and Julie got a ring. I called Missy's the "key to her heart" and Julie's her "promise ring." But they both meant the same thing: Until I walked them down the aisle and gave them away, I held the "key" to their hearts. Their purity was something I counted on and something worth protecting.

When the time was right, they would need to give the "key" to someone else who would love and cherish them—difficult as it is to believe—as much as their dad did. Neither of them forgot that moment.

The story of my interviewing Steven is an example of fairly thorough emotional protection. I was exercising my right to keep Julie from being hurt by this older boy. And although I wasn't angry and avoided any specific threats, I was putting him on notice: "Be careful with this girl. She belongs to a family that cares a great deal for her."

Today, Julie is in her twenties. Am I still protecting her from boys? No. Why? Because my job was to show her *how* to "interview" a boy, by allowing her to enjoy the security of my protection, then teaching her how to do it herself. (See the next chapter on conversation.) Believe it or not, a 21-year-old young woman can have just as much "power" in an interview with a potential suitor as her dad did when she was 16! Just ask a couple of 21-year-old boys.

When my friends heard that I was interviewing Julie's potential dates, I vividly remember them asking me how Julie put up with it. "Man, if I tried that with my daughter's dates, she'd kill me," they said.

No, their daughters probably wouldn't. If they're anything like Julie, they would feel a sense of confidence and security. They would have the assurance that they weren't out in the open alone—that they were still protected by someone who had protected them from day one.

They would also be assured that when there was a problem with something Dad was doing, they could talk to him about it. They could tell him the truth, and he would do his best to listen and not be defensive.

That's why the next chapter is so critical for you to read and understand.

BUILDER'S CHECKLIST

Protecting your girl is your job. It takes a lot of wisdom and patience. Here are a few reminders from this chapter:

1. *Be attentive to the protection seesaw:* As she grows, her need for protection from physical dangers will diminish, but her need for protection from emotional danger will increase. When you're turning her away from the "sharp objects" and "breakable figurines" of life, turn her attention to something else. "Let's play with Legos" or "Let's go for a ride in Daddy's car" are a lot more effective than an adventure-ending *no.*

2. *Childproof your house:* Okay, so it's inconvenient to move everything fragile to an unreachable location, but do it anyway. If you don't, you'll be saying no during every one of her waking hours. Besides, your home decor will be restored in no time.

3. *Take her out . . . a lot:* Yes, there are germs out there. Yes, there are rowdy, block-hurling boys in the church nursery. Take her out anyway. Don't succumb to the temptation—or your wife's—to "protect" your daughter from this stuff. She'll be fine.

4. *Turn loose on time:* Ironically, for some dads, turning their girl loose to "hop down the branch" is tough. They physically over-protect, so their daughters develop an unhealthy, long-term

dependence on them. Then the girls don't learn to make their own good decisions. They can't renew a driver's license or fill out an insurance form. They won't drive a two-hour trip on their own. Don't let this happen. Give your daughter a taste of physical independence when she's small. Sleep-overs at a friend's house or a week of summer camp will help.

5. *Talk about feelings:* As you learn to protect her delicate emotions, also learn to ask about them. "How did that make you feel?" is a magic question. Always support her answer, too. You'll be tempted to argue with her feelings, but don't. If she's angry, let her be angry. Tell her, "If that had happened to me, I would probably be angry, too." If she's hurt, let her be hurt. Never say, "Oh, you don't *really* feel that way, do you?" You'll shut her down, and she'll stop talking to you.

6. *Establish a baby-sitter fund:* No matter how small your salary, always set some money aside for baby-sitters. Your daughter will learn important independence lessons on someone else's watch. Hint: Find *girl* baby-sitters who come from families you know and trust and whose dads have read this book. Another hint: Just as soon as your girl is old enough, get her out there baby-sitting. It's a great way to earn a little extra money, but it's also a chance to learn while she's "teaching." She'll discover just how smart her dad really is.

7. *Interview dates:* Although you'll have a lot of fun telling your friends about this one, it's not a laughing matter to your daughter. Don't let her overhear you bragging about how smart you are to be conducting the interview. This is an intimate thing between you and her. She's trusting you by "letting" you talk to her boyfriends. Don't abuse that privilege. Remember, this interview

is not about your approval of your daughter's choice in boys.
Every boy passes your inspection, regardless. (Gulp.) The very fact
that the interview is going to take place will have a sorting effect
all by itself!

8. *Be as available as you can:* If you have an office job, always let your
   daughter's call "through." If you're in your car a lot, wear a pager
   or carry a cellular phone. This emotional protection thing is about
   good timing. And if you're not there the moment she needs it,
   she'll find someone else . . . possibly someone whose wisdom
   will be inferior to yours.

CHAPTER FOUR

Conversation:
Just keep talking

"To talk to a child, to fascinate her, is much more difficult than

to win an electoral victory. But it is also more rewarding."

COLETTE

Taylor University, my college alma mater, had a dinnertime custom for many years. Folklore had it that, over the years, many women had transferred to other schools because of this tradition.

Every weekday evening, at exactly 6:00, the doors of the dining hall would open, but only for the co-eds. The ladies would stream in, filling every other seat at the round, eight-person tables. They made this processional to the strains of an ancient upright piano in the corner, played, of course, by a music major.

Once the dining hall was exactly half filled, the men were released, set free to prowl the tables, looking for their chosen seat. In selecting where they wanted to sit, they also chose where they *didn't* want to spend their dinner hour. Now do you know why the women hated this practice?

Students waited tables, family style. I'm sure a family atmosphere, with pleasant conversation, is just what the well-intentioned founders of the tradition had wanted to create.

Fortunately, in 1966, this tradition came to an end. The dean had reportedly succumbed to the subtle pressure of 750 club- and torch-toting women.

I remember one dinner in the spring of my freshman year. I was sitting with seven classmates—three men and four women. We were engaged in usual college chatter when someone mentioned the breakup of one of Taylor's "fixture" couples. He was a sophomore;

she was a freshman—one of our own.

All the side conversations at the table stopped. Everyone wanted to hear about couples breaking up. We weren't being hateful, mind you, just "fully informed."

One of the girls gave the report that it was Paula's decision to break off the relationship. "Irreconcilable differences," she said. Paula had loved Michael, but there was just no future in it.

"That's not what I heard," I glibly announced. "I heard that Michael really let her have it. He really hadn't liked her all that much and just told her so. He broke her heart, but, oh well, these things happen." I was a veritable fountain of gossip that evening, and everyone was listening.

When I finished my thorough report, I took a breath and looked up into the faces of my classmates. They were ashen, gazing at me in disbelief. The boys in particular looked sick.

As I looked more closely, I discovered they weren't actually looking at me. They were looking just above me at—you guessed it—our family-style waitress.

I jerked around in my chair to see who had captured their attention. It was Paula.

Paula and I had been friends, often walking to classes together. As a friend, I liked Paula a lot. And until that moment when our eyes locked onto each other's for one very painful second, she had liked me.

I will remember that moment for the rest of my life—what it felt like to be sitting there, trapped in the crossfire of my friend's pain and the disbelieving stares of my seven tablemates. I don't recall ever feeling such embarrassment, such shame.

What I learned that instant was this truth: Words have unbeliev-able power. Clustered together well, they can restore and renew people. They can lift the heart and heal the spirit. They can build the character of the speaker and the esteem of the recipient. But, unfortunately, they can also cause great pain. And once spoken, they can never be unsaid.

The tongue has been accurately compared to the rudder of a ship. With just a little instrument, an entire life can be set on the right course or perilously aimed at an iceberg.

The Crown Jewel

Properly teaching the skills of conversation is the most critical thing a dad must do in building his little girl. The ability of you and your daughter to effectively exchange words—and the feelings they're usually connected to—will provide the bridge between you that will last the rest of your life.

You'll quickly discover that your daughter is more than capable of making noise, even forming words at an early age, but she'll need to learn how to talk. She won't pick this up without some help from you.

Actually, her very first word will be "DaDa." When she says that, you will be absolutely convinced that she's responding to someone's question to her: "Who is the most incredible hunk of human virility on the face of the earth?" You'll be proud—deceived, but proud.

> *The ability of you and your daughter to effectively exchange words—and the feelings they're usually connected to—will provide the bridge between you that will last the rest of your life.*

The World of Words

From the time she's small, read books to your girl. By doing this, you'll introduce her to a world of imagination and truth. Read "fun" books, silly books, nursery rhymes, true-life adventures, and Bible storybooks. Your local library or bookstore will provide you with all the help you need to find some good ones. Without ever having to lecture her, you'll be showing your daughter how wonderful words can be.

Valuing Conversation

From the time she's small, you must also teach your girl to honor conversation—words connecting two human beings. This lesson usually comes in the form of her attempts to interrupt you when you're talking to your wife or another adult.

The first time—and every time—this happens, you must stop talking—midsentence if necessary. Then you look at your girl, and with determination in your voice you say, "Honey, I was talking with your mother. You are not allowed to interrupt us when we're talking. Just as soon as we're finished, you and I can talk. I promise. Do you understand?"

Then, when you and your wife are done, go to your daughter and ask what she has to say. She may have forgotten, and that's okay. Don't shame her with "Hey, if you're going to interrupt me, you'd better have something important to say."

Instead, take a few minutes and have a conversation. And whatever you do, protect this little talk from any interruptions, even one that comes from an adult! As you're talking to your girl, also make sure your eyes connect. Don't let your mind wander, either. Hang in there as long as you possibly can.

By listening carefully while she's speaking, you will be telling her nonverbally that conversation is very important. You'll also be communicating your love for her.

How Many Cows Can You Count Over There?

When your girl is small, there really aren't that many interesting things you can talk about. You live in a world that's foreign to her. You've got pressure at work and are struggling to make ends meet. She's got a dolly who scraped her knee. So you'll have to find some things to discuss and places to discuss them.

No problem.

A good friend taught me a fathering lesson early in my parenting. "On the weekends, never go anywhere alone," he told me. Simple advice with wonderful consequences. Taking his counsel, I rarely went out for errands on the weekend alone. I took Missy or Julie along.

As we were driving, I would ask questions. "Look over there in that field. Have you ever seen so many cows? I wonder how many there are." My daughter would look and start counting.

Or we'd play games. "Between here and the store," I'd say, "let's count how many trucks we pass." Or, "If you were an animal in the zoo, what animal would you like to be?"

Early in our lives together, we built a connection of words that inextricably bound us together.

The Gift That Keeps on Giving

Several years ago, our company posted a classified ad to find some-one to fill an open position. After a full and exhausting day of meeting prospective employees, one thing was clear: Some of those people had been taught how to carry on a conversation, and some hadn't. Those who knew the art had a shot at the job. Those who didn't, didn't.

Teaching your girl how to talk is like giving her a wonderful gift, one she'll enjoy for the rest of her life.

In describing good conversation, Dr. James Dobson uses the helpful illustration of playing catch with a tennis ball. When you want to speak to someone, you "throw" the person a question. When he or she answers, the person is "throwing" a response back. Once you've caught the response, you "toss" another question.

Several years ago, we had a houseguest who stayed with us for nearly three months. The company I worked for had just hired Rick, and he was staying with us until the school year was over and his wife and children could join him. Although Rick was a wonderful guy, he tended toward shyness, especially around strangers.

One night, Bobbie and I were going out to meet friends for dinner, so we left Missy and Julie—then 14 and 11—home to eat dinner with Rick. Scared that they would sit there staring silently at each other for an hour or so, the girls came to me for help.

Fortunately, I remembered Dr. Dobson's illustration. "I want you to picture yourself sitting at the table with Rick," I told them. "He won't be able to see the stack of tennis balls you've hidden in your lap. After you say the blessing for dinner, I want one of you—Julie, you go first—to reach down, pick up one of the tennis balls, and throw it at Rick."

Knowing from experience that good table manners were important to me, they looked shocked. "Dad," Missy exclaimed, "you're not serious."

After just a moment of making them think I really meant for this dinner to turn into Wimbledon, I assured them I was kidding. "Well, kind of," I finally said.

I told them about the "game" of conversation. "When you want to talk with people, you *throw* them a question, just like a tennis ball. And, hopefully, they'll *catch* it and *throw* it back with an answer. You catch the ball and throw another question back.

"Of course," I explained, "you never actually tell anyone you're playing a game of catch. You keep that to yourself."

This was beginning to sound like fun, eating dinner and playing a game at the same time. I explained that "tennis balls" may be questions like, "Who was your favorite teacher in grade school? Who was your best friend in junior high? What sports did you like when you were growing up?"

"What if Rick doesn't throw the ball back?" Missy alertly asked.

"That's okay, Missy," I said. "If he doesn't return the ball, just throw him another one."

The girls were ready for dinner—and Rick.

Bobbie and I got home late that night. The report of tennis balls at dinnertime would have to wait for a few more hours. However, the next morning, our two little girls were bursting with the news of last night's dinner. "How did it go?" I asked.

Missy's eyes were wide. "Dad," she said, "by the time we were finished with dinner, Rick was *covered* with tennis balls!"

Teach your girl how to carry on a conversation. Role play and practice. Teach her to listen so she can ask a question that follows what you've just said. Show her how it works.

"Tell me about your recess today at school, Julie," I'd start the rehearsal.

"Brandon fell off the jungle gym," she'd say.

"Wow, did he hurt himself?"

"I think so."

"How do you know?"

"He cried."

"What did Mrs. Bond do?"

"She took Brandon to the school nurse."

"Then what happened?"

"The nurse called Brandon's mother."

"I'll bet you felt sorry for Brandon . . ."

The secret of an effective conversation is to never catch the ball and stick it in your pocket.

If, after Julie had told me that Brandon had cracked his head on the playground, I had only said "That's too bad" or "I'm sorry for Brandon," I would have been putting the ball in my pocket. Instead, however, I threw it back with a question: "Wow, did he hurt himself?"

Forgive me if going through this elementary exercise is insulting to your intelligence, but I know your natural tendency will be to stick tennis balls in your pocket. And you'll miss the opportunities that present themselves to show your little girl exactly how to make a conversation work.

"That's a Pretty Picture, Honey"

Little children are famous for indecipherable drawings. But instead of saying "That's nice, Sweetie" or "What is it?" you need to say, "Tell me about your picture, Jennifer."

Then Jennifer describes what *she* sees, which, of course, is all that matters. As she talks, you listen—carefully—so you can say, "That's so interesting that you colored that pony orange. Can you tell me why you chose such an interesting color?"

Your girl is learning to speak, to accurately express what's inside. And you're learning to listen so you can catch a glimpse of who this little girl really is.

Then when Jennifer comes home from high school after a verbal bout with one of her classmates, you say, "Tell me about Mindy." Listen carefully. Next follow up with something like, "It's awful that Mindy would say something so mean. I wonder why she would talk like that."

Unfortunately, a 16-year-old Jennifer will never talk to you that way unless, when she was small and the stakes weren't as high, you taught her how.

"It's Nice to Meet You, Dr. Holland"

Our home in Waco, Texas, was a full 100 miles from a major airport. Because my work required a lot of travel, I was forced to fly a commuter between Waco and Dallas.

You've been on those planes where there's no door between the cockpit and the passengers. For the most part, I prefer not knowing what's actually going on up there, just as I'd rather not know what really happens in a restaurant kitchen. But in this case, there was no choice.

Fastened to the steering column with a thick rubber band was a laminated card. At the top of the card were the words "Pre-flight checklist." And before the plane left its moorings in front of the terminal, the passengers got a look at the captain as he went down his checklist, making sure he hadn't forgotten anything.

Less than a century ago, children were taught the art of conversation in school. They were given a checklist of how to talk—what to say, what not to say, how to greet an adult, and the use of the words "Sir" and "Ma'am." But most schools today won't provide your girl with such a checklist, so you're going to have to do this yourself.

Today's lesson is on meeting grown-ups. Remember, this isn't going to happen properly without some instruction—a checklist to "fasten to her mind" with a thick rubber band.

You begin this lesson by telling her that there will be times when you'll want to introduce her to your friends. You remind her that she's important to you and you want your friends to meet such a special girl.

Then you describe a typical situation. You're out with her, and one of your friends walks up to the two of you. This happens a lot on weekends—grocery stores and Home Depot—since you've got your girl with you on all your errands. You say to your friend, "Hey, Gary, have you met Julie?"

"No, I don't believe I have," your friend answers.

You look at your little girl and say these words: "Julie, I'd like you to meet my friend, Dr. Holland. Dr. Holland, this is Julie."

Julie looks at Gary—not at his shoes, at his *eyes*—holds out her hand, and says, "It's nice to meet you, Dr. Holland."

Gary, without any prompting from you, will take her hand, shake it, and faint, out cold on the floor. No, actually, he'll lean over, take her hand, and say something like, "Well, it's nice to meet you, too, Julie. You're such a polite little girl."

You may be saying, "Come on. This sounds awfully rigid. After all, we're not living in Victorian England. I prefer letting my daughter be her spontaneous little self."

Okay, but you're missing a golden opportunity to give your girl the gift of esteem that comes from receiving an adult's approval. If you follow my plan, she gets to hear a grown-up's kind word of affirmation, the reassurance that she *is* a special girl, from some-one—a big person—she's just met.

I encourage you to practice this one until she gets it. And if she slips up in an actual meeting, take the opportunity—once Dr. Holland is no longer around—to correct the mistakes. Be sure to affirm the parts she got right: "That was good, Honey, but you didn't look right at Dr. Holland when you said, 'Nice to meet you, Dr. Holland.' The next time, look at him when you're speaking to him."

No Children's Table at Our House

When I was a kid, holidays were filled with great family conversation, especially around the dinner table. Looking back on those wonderful feasts, I recall that my mother always did her best to add on to our primary dining room table rather than arrange a separate table in the kitchen for little people.

I can remember because I was often recruited to help set up a card table or two next to the main table, extending it well into the living room. The card tables were usually a different height than the formal table, but for my mother, it wasn't a problem. "Since we're a family," she'd say, "we're all going to eat together. All ages at the big table. No *kids' table* in the other room."

She was right. As children, my three brothers, two sisters, and I learned the importance of conversation. We learned that the dinner table wasn't a conveyor belt covered with food. We were taught that sitting down to a meal was an important time of discussion, of listening to others and having them listen to us.

And when we were finished eating, that didn't mean we were no longer needed at the table. Being excused early was rare. Today, I'm grateful for that.

What Was Your Favorite Thing Today?

If you and your wife have more than one child, you'll discover that conversational ability is stronger in some than in others. Your older child may be more deliberate in her talking, making each of her words count. Your younger child may be spontaneous and talkative, never leaving you to wonder what she's thinking. Family conversations may be lopsided, with one child completely dominating — so maybe she'll run for Congress some day and make you proud — and the other holding back.

Bobbie invented a way to create balanced table conversation when the girls were small. She would routinely suggest that we "go around the table and tell each other our happiest thing and our saddest thing today."

No one was exempt. I had to talk about my day along with everyone else. From the girls, we heard about neighborhood toughs and hurt feelings. We listened to each report. One summer, for almost a month, Julie's happiest thing was the neighbor's new sliding board. And we did our best to listen as though we had never heard about it before.

These times of good talk with your children are the stuff with which relationships are built. And they should be protected as though they were precious. Difficult as it is to coordinate your schedules to have dinner together these days, I would still strongly encourage you to fight for it—two or three times a week, minimum.

Several months ago, Bobbie and I spent the night with friends in Atlanta. They have three beautiful children, small and active. Over breakfast, Darren asked me, "What's the most important thing I can do for our children?"

I looked around their impeccably decorated home. As a successful attorney, Darren had been able to provide his family with every comfort imaginable. The question was one I had never been asked before, so I took a moment to think about my answer.

"Teach your kids to talk to you," I finally replied. "Open conversation will be your lifeline. It will keep your kids from emotionally hiding from you and your wife. It will allow you to learn who your children really are and give you a vehicle to tell them about yourself. Teaching your children the art of conversation will introduce them to a world of other adults who will honor them because of their ability to talk and listen."

Down with Pronouns

There's another thing about conversation that may be helpful to your family. When talking about another member of the family, especially in that person's presence, avoid the use of pronouns.

Here's the way it works: You're at the table, and your children are talking about each other. In fact, let's say your daughter is reporting—tattling—on her brother's activities. If you allow her to, she'll refer to her brother as "he," as in, "He barged into my bedroom without knocking!" As long as her brother can condescendingly be referred to as a faceless "he," there will be little chance for amicable resolution.

So when your daughter says "he," stop her. Tell her to use her brother's name. Ask her to repeat what she has just said, using "David" instead of "he." And even if this little spat will need to end with David making a full confession, he'll still have a little self-esteem left because of the respectful way he's being referred to.

As Dale Carnegie said about using a person's name when talking to—or about—him, the sound of a person's own name is the most beautiful thing he can hear. Teach your family to use people's names.

A Pile of Rocks and Other Important Memories

In the Old Testament, the story is told of Jacob on his way to find a wife. In the night, he had an encounter with an angel. Without going into detail here, let's just say it was a serious conversation! The next morning, as Jacob was preparing to break camp and move on, he decided to build a little monument—a simple pile of rocks—to that conversation.

Although it's not recorded, I wouldn't be surprised if, when Jacob returned home with Rachel on his arm, he passed by that pile of rocks and told his bride about the night he spent talking with an angel.

There's a restaurant in Waco that will, for all our lives, be a "stack of rocks" for Missy, Julie, and me. Harold Waites' was one of those old-time diners where the burgundy-vinyl-covered booth benches were repaired with duct tape, the imitation walnut Formica on the tables was worn to white at the corners, smokers were everywhere, and the waitresses all called you "Honey." It was a place where, maybe twice a month for the five years we lived in Texas, the three of us would have Saturday morning breakfast together.

And because there are still restaurants like that all over America, every time Missy and Julie see an old diner, they remember our Saturday morning talks. To them it's like Jacob's pile of rocks.

Dots Over Breakfast

One of the dangers of such breakfast meetings is that you may have a hard time finding things to talk about, especially *before* your scrambled eggs arrive. In fact, when you and your girl find your special place, you may see other dads—who have been to a seminar or read a book—with their children. Sometimes, if you look closely, you may see dads reading the newspaper or talking with *their* friends who are *also* out to breakfast with their kids.

Flag on the play. Fifteen-yard penalty.

The last thing you want your girl to recall about this special place is sitting there bored to death while you read box scores or talked to your friends about the stock market.

What we did was play "dots." You might remember playing this game when you were a kid. You take a piece of paper and lay out a series of dots in rows and columns.

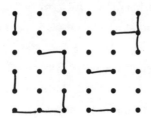

Each of you takes a turn connecting two dots, either horizontally or vertically.

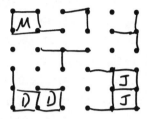

The trick is to be able to complete a box with your line. And when you do, you put your initial inside the box. Every time you write your initial, you get to connect two more dots. The most initials when all the possible lines are drawn wins.

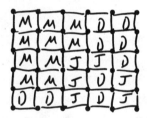

You can come up with another game, but this one was great fun for us, and it didn't make any annoying, electronic beeping sounds!

The important thing is that it gave us something to do every time we went out to breakfast. While we were connecting dots, we would talk. Finally—and please don't miss this one—it was the only time we ever played dots. There were other times when we were tempted to get out a piece of paper and play dots, but we resisted the temptation. "Dots" was only for Harold Waites'. In fact, the girls eventually started calling our breakfast place "Harold Dots." The game was another "rock pile" that will, for the rest of the girls' lives, represent one simple thing: good conversation.

For Girls Only?

You may be wondering, especially if you also have a son, "Isn't it important to teach a boy how to talk, too?"

Yes, of course it is. However, there are several reasons why I place such importance on this between you and your daughter. Among these are the fact that, for the most part, girls have the capacity of becoming more adept at conversation than boys at an early age. Since you're being a good conversation instructor for her, she will "teach" others—especially boys—how to do the same. As she begins to discover the world of other men besides you, she'll be able to make better judgments about who's compatible as a potential friend and who's not.

> *As she begins to discover the world of other men besides you, she'll be able to make better judgments about who's compatible as a potential friend and who's not.*

As she "throws tennis balls" at boys, she'll learn who they are and what's important to them. She will less likely be surprised by a boy's errant belief system or broken moral compass if she has been engaged in meaningful conversation with him.

Because she has learned the art of good conversation, your daughter will also be less likely to get caught in compromising physical situations. First, assuming that boys will nearly always be the aggressors, she'll know how to openly express her commitments to purity and her fears of the consequences of premarital intimate contact. Second, young lovebirds usually choose between talk and the backseat. They don't do both simultaneously. My preference would be for my daughter to talk!

Taking Words Back

This chapter opened with a lesson I learned about the power of words. As adults, you and I know that once something has been spoken, it simply cannot be retrieved.

Listening to talk-radio is a good reminder of this. The host's microphone is "live." When something is spoken, it shoots out on the airwaves and cannot be pulled back. It's toothpaste squeezed from a tube. It can never be replaced.

But you can always tell professionals from amateurs on the radio by how they deal with mistakes. An amateur will catch himself, issue a few "uh's" and "um's," then fall all over himself apologizing for having said the wrong thing. He may even nervously laugh at what he has done.

A professional will quickly acknowledge the mistake, fix it, then go on: "The Chicago Bears scored three touchdowns in the second inning, rather, the second *quarter*, of their battle with the Green Bay Packers . . ."

Even as a seasoned conversationalist, you're going to make mistakes. You're going to say foolish and inappropriate things. Don't ignore them. But don't grovel and blubber, either.

Acknowledge your blunder, confess it, correct it, and move on with the conversation. Getting good at this will help you teach your girl how to do the same thing when she fails.

The Importance of Saying "I'm Sorry"

Because Julie was old enough to push the lawn mower, my weeklong business trip and the ankle-deep grass surrounding our house gave her all she needed to decide to surprise me.

Driving home from the airport, I was reviewing the chores waiting at home. *My grass must be knee deep by now. I certainly hope none of the neighbor kids have gotten lost in my front yard.*

But when I pulled into the driveway, I couldn't believe my eyes. Someone had *already* cut the grass, and it looked pretty good. I say "pretty good" because I have this thing about my lawn. My goal is to have it look like a major league infield. In addition to collecting the clippings, I cross-hatch my mowing at a perfect 45 degree angle, alternating the direction each time I cut it. I also slice along the grass next to the driveway and flower beds with my edge trimmer. It looks like my freshly waxed high-school flattop the whole way around.

Whoever had mowed my yard hadn't caught the clippings or edged around the beds. Here and there were clumps of cut grass. Don't get me wrong—I was glad someone had taken the initiative to do the yard. It's just that it wasn't exactly the way I would have done it.

When I walked into the house, I could tell immediately that it was Julie who had mowed the lawn. She had that aren't-you-proud-of-me look all over her face. I hugged her and thanked her for doing such a thoughtful thing. Proudly, I didn't say a thing about the loose clumps of grass or the scraggly edges. But I did change immediately into my work clothes and go outside to *re-cut* the grass . . . properly.

When Julie looked out to see what I was doing, she was crushed. Although I had *said* nothing about my displeasure, what I *did* that summer afternoon "spoke" volumes. My eccentric foolishness had crushed my daughter's spirit.

That evening, Bobbie took me aside to tell me how Julie had reacted. The pain that my silent criticism had inflicted on her was far worse than a little extra "thatch" in my grass or unmanicured edges.

In my haste to get it just right, I had missed a chance to celebrate my daughter's honest attempt to please her dad. And I had hurt her feelings in the process. Finally realizing that, I went to her, said I was sorry, and asked for her pardon. Fortunately, she forgave me for being such an insensitive jerk.

When you blow it with your daughter, as I did that time, be quick to apologize and ask for her forgiveness.

A Lesson from a Jackhammer

Believe it or not, the first time I used a jackhammer, I learned a key lesson about the importance of conversation.

The thing that drives a jackhammer is air under tremendous pressure. This pressurized air comes from a compressor that, with the help of a gasoline engine, fills a tank to which a hose from the jackhammer is connected. You've seen contractors pulling these compressors around behind their pickups.

When the tank is filling with air, you can hear the gas engine running full speed. But when the tank is full, the engine seems to slip into neutral, and you can hear a loud hissing sound. This sound comes from a small valve attached to the air tank. What it does is simple: When the tank is packed tightly with air, so tightly that any more air would blow up the whole thing, sending the entire crew to that great coffee break in the sky, that valve tells the engine to take a break, then releases some of the air.

That little, inexpensive pressure valve preserves the life of an expensive piece of equipment and the lives of the people working close by. What a nice idea!

Conversation does the same thing. Used properly, it can release the pressure that builds in every relationship. It's that magic little device that gives people the opportunity to talk about frustrations or fears without allowing pressure to build, expensive "compressors" to explode, and people to be irreparably harmed.

A Gift That Will Be Returned

If you give your girl the gift of conversational skills, you will receive the gift back many times in the years to come. Let me illustrate.

On my forty-fourth birthday, I got the phone call every entrepreneur dreads. The man on the other end had a brief message: "Robert, we have to call the note on your business loan. I know what this means, and I'm sorry. I'm a man under authority, and I have to do what I have to do."

After we hung up, I sat there stunned. My five-year-old dream had come to an end. I took a deep breath, walked into my business partner's office, and gave him the news. Our eyes welled up as we realized the impact of this news.

A few minutes later, our whole staff was together, not having any idea what they were about to hear. My partner and I had done our best to protect them from the rough seas our business had encountered, but now we had to tell them they were out of work and should start looking for other jobs.

I went back to my office, closed the door, and called Bobbie. When I heard her voice, I broke down, sobbing uncontrollably. Once I gathered my composure, I told her what had happened. "We've lost everything, Honey," I said. "I can't believe it."

Over the next few weeks, I had to make many painful calls. One of the most difficult was to Missy, by then a college sophomore. After telling her about closing my business, I let her know we wouldn't be able to continue paying for her out-of-town, private college education after the current semester.

Her response was quick and full of grown-up resolve. "That's okay, Daddy," she said. "I love this school, but if I need to work for a year to help us make ends meet, I'll do it. And whatever you do, don't pull Julie out of Brentwood Academy. I can help with her tuition if I need to."

The rest of the conversation was filled with tenderness and affirmation. As we hung up, I thanked Missy for her encouragement. I told her how grateful I was that she still believed in me, and how much I loved her.

For those moments, our roles had been reversed. I had needed my daughter more than she needed me. And because I had taught her the art of listening and conversing when she was small, she could now return the gift to me.

Give your daughter that same gift.

BUILDER'S CHECKLIST

Conversation is absolutely foundational in your relationship with your daughter. But it won't happen automatically. Here are a few reminders from this chapter:

1. *Show your daughter that words are wonderful:* Read to your girl even before you think she can understand a thing. It will create in her a love for words and an appreciation for your bringing the world to her through books.

2. *Engage in honoring conversation:* Don't let her interrupt when you're in a conversation with someone else. This includes when you're on the phone. When she interrupts, stop talking immediately, get her attention, and remind her that you're speaking with someone else. Then when you're finished with your conversation, get back to her right away and find out what she wanted to talk about.

3. *Take her along:* Try not to run any errands without your girl next to you in the front seat. While you're riding along, get conversation started with questions about her surroundings: "How many

cows?" "How many buses?" It's easy.

4. *Play verbal tennis:* Teach your girl how conversation works. "Throw" her a question, and teach her how to "throw" back a response with another question. Try to avoid "sticking the ball in your pocket" too soon. Also, be sure to listen carefully.

5. *Ask good questions:* "Tell me about your picture." "What an interesting combination you're wearing. Tell me why you chose such an unusual outfit."

6. *Teach her to say, "Nice to meet you, Dr. Holland":* Teach her how to properly meet someone. Practice until she gets it right.

7. *Please pass the conversation:* Don't be so quick to excuse your daughter from the dinner table. Expect her to stay and contribute to the conversation, or just listen to others talking. Be careful to include her as much as possible so it's not too painful!

8. *Pile up the rocks:* Look for places to call your own: An old diner in your town for breakfast or a city park for walking. It doesn't have to be fancy or expensive; it just needs to be.

9. *Apologize for words poorly spoken:* Because you're normal, you're going to say the wrong thing at the wrong time. You're going to hurt people's feelings, including your daughter's. Show her what it sounds like to hear her dad correct his words and, if necessary, ask her forgiveness for the error.

10. *Realize that all this will take time and patience:* But the rewards of having a girl grow up to be one of your best friends are incredible. And conversation is how this relationship will grow.

Affection:
Daddy, hold me

"Praise is well, compliment is well, but affection—that is the

last and final and most precious reward that any man can win."

MARK TWAIN

Biology was my favorite subject in high school. It was the only class I had where I could do something with my hands—not counting taking notes or turning pages. Foolishly, I didn't take any "shop" classes in high school.

I remember what it felt like walking into Mr. Dusak's biology classroom at Wheaton Community High. I can still smell the odor—not Mr. Dusak, just the formaldehyde and various other chemicals. Standing in the doorway in my memory, I can see the lab tables to my left and the blackboard to my right.

At the right end of the blackboard hung a huge, life-sized, full-color flip chart of a man. This chart had several pages, each containing a diagram of one of the "systems" inside the man. There was the skeletal system, the respiratory system, the digestive system, the reproductive system (our favorite—we were sophomore boys), and the nervous system.

Maybe you had a chart like that in your biology class, too.

If you did, can you remember what the nervous system looked like? It showed the brain, which looked like oatmeal with deep wrinkles, the spinal column, and all the nerves coming out from it that looked like little rivers and streams.

Question: Where was the largest congregation of nerves, once they'd left the spinal column? In other words, where was the biggest collection of nerves that would make for the highest degree of sensitivity?

It was in the hands and fingers.

One Man's Painful Lesson

On his wedding day a long time ago, my friend Chuck Aycock was painting a house at the top of a long extension ladder. No one knows exactly why he wasn't out looking for a pair of dark socks—the *only* thing a man has to do on his wedding day—but he wasn't. He was painting a two-story house.

Suddenly, the ladder began to fall, sliding along the gutter. It started slowly, but the farther it slid, the faster it went. Spontaneously, Chuck dropped the paint and brush and grabbed the gutter.

Time out. Picture a cross-section of a gutter. Along the top, front edge, the part that's visible from the street, the sheet metal bends around to give a smooth, finished look. However, the gutter edge comes to a stop right after it makes that turn, providing a veritable catch-basin for every falling leaf in your county.

Well, as my friend Chuck discovered when his ladder was slipping toward earth, that edge is also like a 40-foot blade running along the front of the house. With the combination of the speed of his lateral movement and that sharp, unfinished, sheet-metal edge, grabbing the gutter wasn't the smartest thing he could have done. Knowing he really didn't have much choice, I don't blame him for doing that. It's just that, looking back, he probably should have opted for a broken leg, because he fell to the ground anyway.

What happened was that the skin on the front of his eight fingers was peeled back from the first knuckle to the tips of each one. Do you feel sorry for Chuck? Do your fingers ache just reading about this? Okay, I'll hurry on.

Because he was painting a house instead of looking for dark socks, Chuck got to go through the rest of his wedding day—and a few days after—with his hands completely bandaged. He did *not* break his leg. What's more, because of the throbbing pain caused by leaving his hands hanging at his side, he had to hold them up.

This wedding happened a long time before videotape was invented, but it would be an interesting thing to see again. At the front of the church, you've got four or five pretty bridesmaids on the left side. They're holding lovely bouquets. And four or five handsome groomsmen are on the right, standing very still, not locking their knees and keeping their hands *to their sides.*

You've got flowers and candles tastefully placed across the front of the sanctuary and the minister facing the bride and bridegroom. You can see the back of the bride's gown, all beautifully decorated with sequins and lace, flowing back down the aisle.

And then you've got Chuck, signaling a touchdown.

The Power of Touch

When Chuck first told me that story, I remembered the chart in Mr. Dusak's biology room. I remembered the collection of nerves at the fingertips, and I realized how important the sense of touch is.

In fact, although you'll never find this on any chart, it almost seems as if there's so much feeling in the hands and fingers that there ought to be a little connector—a nerve, a blood vessel, maybe a clear, plastic tube—between the hands and the heart.

> *To your daughter, touching is the key to her heart.*

Way back in the Old Testament, when the serpent was trying to get Eve to disobey God, she told him that God had told Adam to not even *touch* the fruit.

You can look for yourself, but God never told Adam that. He only told him not to eat it. But to Eve—a woman—*touching* the fruit was just the same as picking it and eating it.

To your daughter, touching is the key to her heart. And, as you'll see, there are two kinds of "touching" you'll use with your girl: physical and verbal.

A Stout Warning

As you read the rest of this chapter, your mind will naturally be drawn to an important issue. "Touching" your daughter falls into two categories: appropriate physical and verbal touching and *inappropriate* physical and verbal touching.

Unfortunately, our newspapers repeatedly remind us that there are fathers who don't know the difference. We see photos of them being shamefully ushered off to prison. We hear horrific accounts from grown women who are dealing with the unthinkable trauma of having been violated by fathers who disregarded their own consciences.

If you're afraid you may be such a father, please stop reading this book and seek the help of a trained professional.

Physical Touching

I'm going to assume that if you're still reading, you know the difference between appropriate and inappropriate. And if I could sit down with you right now and look into your eyes, I'd tell you not to miss what follows. No, I'd beg you not to miss it.

Hold your daughter when she's a baby, and stroke her face with your hand. Hold her hand when you walk with her. Visit her room just before she goes to sleep, and kiss her good night. Hug her with your whole arms—wrap her up like a blanket. Let her heart know—through that little connector between her toucher and her heart—that she is absolutely secure in her daddy's arms.

All this takes some extra time. You cannot do any of this meaningful touching on the fly. You have to slow down to make it mean something.

Both of my maternal grandparents and my paternal grandmother lived their final years in a retirement center in south-central Pennsylvania. The first time we visited the "home," the director took us on a tour. We were impressed with the tasteful decor and the good-natured, professional staff.

But the thing I'll never forget was a large room we walked into. Probably measuring 20 by 50 feet, it was literally filled with rocking chairs. The director explained that there was a day-care center for preschoolers right in the middle of the home. The playground was the atrium surrounded by the residents' rooms, so throughout the day, the voices of children wafted through the complex.

Each day, right after lunch, it was "quiet time" for the kids. They would file into this large, rocking-chair-filled room, looking for their special friend. Crawling up on their adopted lap, they would experience the touch—and, therefore, the love—of an elderly person with lots of it to give.

"Visiting this room during quiet time is an awesome thing," the director explained. "The room is intentionally darkened, and the shadowed back-and-forth squeak of the rockers and soft sounds of talking or humming make it feel like a holy place. It's almost like walking into the hushed narthex of a great European cathedral."

The Nobel Prize for good ideas goes to the person who came up with that one.

Eavesdropping on that scene would probably turn up little in the way of lectures about life. You would not have heard, "When I was a little boy, I . . ." or "You know, I'm glad you asked me that question, because . . ." But the power of touch was wrapping itself into the souls of those little children, assuring them they were worthy of someone's love, that life need not be frightening, that good is stronger than evil, and that love is best communicated in a touch.

Touch your daughter. Stop running, take a minute, and touch your girl.

On the Road Again

In the summer of 1978, I started running for exercise. I had been on the track team in junior high, but in the intervening years I had lost my interest in the "sport." Jim Fixx had just published *The Complete Book of Running,* shoe makers were beginning to discover that there was more to life than low-cut Converse All-Stars, and I was off.

When we moved to our present house in 1991, tucked among a few Tennessee foothills, I found a wonderful five-and-a-half-mile winding road. It provided just enough terrain and scenery to make it interesting, but not so much that I'd become discouraged by its difficulty.

The only thing I didn't like about this run was the dog living between miles three and four. He was a Husky, gray with black eyes and mean—very angry and mean. Sometimes he'd be standing on the road as I approached. At other times he'd be hiding behind a tree or a barn, just waiting to charge me, barking and snarling as if I were some specially flavored dog chow.

I hated this dog. I plotted his demise. I thought of driving up the road late some night and shooting his lights out. Then I decided to buy a can of Mace. *Yes, I can spray the Mace in his eyes, and he'll never chase me again. I'll get that vicious animal. I'll teach him who's boss around these hills.*

But before I had a chance to buy the Mace, I bumped into the guy who lives at the end of our street. Although we had never run together, I knew he was a runner, too. I asked if he knew about "my" five-and-a-half-mile course. He said he did. I asked if he knew about the Husky. He said he did. I asked if the dog had frightened him the way he frightened me. He said, "Well, at first he did."

"At first?" I returned.

"Yes, until one day I decided to stop running for a moment. I squatted down in the middle of the road and petted him. The dog rolled over on his back, begging me to scratch his tummy. Now I look forward to seeing him when I run."

I felt so stupid. This "angry" dog just wanted a friend, someone to stop running long enough to stroke his fur and pat his head.

Stop running and touch your daughter. Touching connects. Touching seals a peace. Touching is like glue, bonding you together for the rest of your lives.

When you take your daughter along with you in your car on those weekend errands, every once in a while reach over and pat her knee. Don't make it a big deal; just touch her. When you're sitting next to her in church, gently squeeze her hand. You don't even need to look at her. In fact, this squeeze will be like your little secret "conversation." Just you and her.

Secret Connections

My mother taught us something her mother had taught her—kind of a "squeeze language." The way it works is that you take your daughter's hand—church is a great place for this—and tenderly squeeze it four times in a row. Then, she squeezes your hand three times. You return the three squeezes with two of your own. She ends this silent "conversation" with one final strong squeeze of your hand.

The interpretation of this squeezing conversation is, "Do you love me?" Four words, four squeezes. Her answer is, "Yes, I do." Three words, three squeezes. Your response is, "How much?" And her final answer comes in a strong squeeze.

You might be thinking, *Come on. Isn't this a little silly—touching, patting, squeezing? "Talking" in squeeze language? Couldn't I just buy her something?*

No, it's not only *not* silly, but it may even be one of the most precious things you'll ever have between you and your daughter. It will be something you'll never outgrow. It will be the only "words" you'll be able to speak at awkward or painful moments. And the older *you* get, the more love you'll feel in touches coming *from* your daughter. Of course, she will have learned this from you.

The Fall of the Wall

In the mid-1980s, when the Berlin Wall was about to crumble, I saw a news account of East Germans boarding a train to visit friends and family living in West Germany. As the train pulled away from the station, those people were throwing money out the window. I can still see thousands of swirling bills following the train as it wound its way to freedom.

Why were they doing such a foolish thing? Why would anyone throw their money away?

It was simple. Where they were going, their money no longer worked. In fact, when they would eventually return to their homes, that money wouldn't ever work again.

Too often, in their genuine attempts to demonstrate affection to their daughters, dads buy them things. "I'm not too good at this gentleness stuff, so I'll go splurge a little and show her how much I really care."

Sorry, but though that strategy sounds logical—maybe because it worked with you!—it doesn't work with your daughter. The place where you want your relationship with her to go, that "currency" doesn't work.

When we lived in Texas, I decided to bite the financial bullet and put a swimming pool in our backyard. Missy was 12 and Julie was 9. On Memorial Day 1983, I enjoyed our pool as I never thought I could. It's a day I'll vividly remember for the rest of my life.

We had worked hard the previous fall and winter to redo our backyard. And even though we had the pool professionally dug and poured, the girls and I had done a lot of work ourselves—200 feet of retaining wall using 7,000 bricks, 11 tons of rock, and 120 batches of mortar! We had also built a pool house and deck. On May 30, we were ready to enjoy our pool.

Like it was yesterday, I can remember the three of us (Bobbie used the pool for exercise, not, primarily, for play) splashing, racing, holding our breath underwater, laughing, tumbling, and dunking each other until, at the end of the afternoon, we collapsed from exhaustion.

It was a day of touching, all in the spirit of fun and play, but a day of my "telling" my girls that I loved them, that I couldn't be happier with God's gift, and that, for the rest of their lives, they were going to be okay.

Touching does all of that. I'm not kidding.

Rub a Dub Dub

One of the gifts I gave my wife when the girls were small was taking responsibility for giving baths. Once they had outgrown the kitchen sink, leaning over the bathtub became my job. Actually, it wasn't that bad.

I remember sliding them back and forth in the slippery tub, pretending they were hockey pucks. I can picture little "hats" we made with the soap suds. I can feel the weight of Missy's or Julie's head in my hand as I washed their hair under the stream of water coming from the spigot. "It isn't too hot, is it?" I always gave them a washcloth to hold over their eyes to make it as painless as possible.

As I lifted them out of the tub, they would kick the excess water from their feet. Then standing them in front of me as I sat on the closed commode, I towel-dried their slippery bodies and wet hair.

Although I initially thought of this job as a chore, looking back on it now, I realize it was a gift to me, too—to have the privilege of making a dad's touch as normal as breathing and sleeping. Touching inextricably bonded my daughters to me and me to them.

How old is your daughter before she lets you know she's too old for her daddy to give her a bath? She *will* let you know. This communiqué may come as early as when she's three or four years old. It may not happen until she's five or six. But when it happens, you're done with bathing that instant. That's okay. The fun experience has deposited plenty of tender security in your daughter's memory bank.

Please hear me on this one. Touch your daughter.

One final word about touching: Do not *use* touching to get something from your daughter. It won't work. If you try to touch or hold her after you've wronged her in some way or when you're in a conflict, she'll yank back from you. She has a right to do that.

Touching only "works" when you've talked out a tough situation or when things are in good shape between you and her. Touching is the signature scrawled at the end of an agreement to seal it. Touching is not a scheme to get your way. It won't work.

Touching with Your Words

"Touching words"—statements of affection—*are* the agreement that physical touch seals. They define exactly what it is you're thinking or feeling. They leave no room for doubt.

These words can be written or spoken. My wife taught me about this.

When the girls were in school, Bobbie packed their lunches every day. In each girl's brown bag, Bobbie always included a small luncheon napkin. *On* the napkin, she'd write a note. Every day she would say something special. It could have been as general as "I love you today" or as specific as "I'm praying that you do well on your science test."

The girls regularly told us that their friends would ask, "What did your mom write today?" These verbal "touchings" made the girls proud. Occasionally, Bobbie would ask me to write the napkin message for the day, but I can't take any credit for this great idea. It was all hers.

Note: If you have a son and you or your wife pack his lunch, don't do napkin notes. I won't go into the "why's" of this directive; you'll just have to trust me.

Early on, we learned the fun of leaving notes everywhere. Notes left on pillows and tucked into shoes and suitcases are powerful word "touchings."

Several years ago, I saw a television ad for Hallmark cards. The scene was a young woman, probably 16, opening the envelope of a greeting in her dad's presence. He was sitting in a masculine-looking, leather, wingback chair, proudly looking on.

The girl carefully read the outside of the card, then opened it to the inside message. Next she spoke to her dad in words I'll never forget. She said, "Oh, Daddy, thank you. You have never said that to me before."

I'm sure the advertising copywriters thought they were doing the right thing to create this hypothetical moment on film, but it infuriated me. I can remember shouting at my TV, "What did you say? Did you say your dad has never spoken those words to you? Never?"

When I calmed down, it dawned on me that, until his daughter was 16 years old, this poor dad had never basked in the luxury of "speaking" affection to his daughter. He had never experienced the thrill of watching her eyes dance when he spoke words to her like, "I love you, Cindy. In fact, I'm sure I'm the luckiest dad on the face of the earth to have a daughter as precious as you."

Just as physical touching takes a slowing-down moment, meaningful words take a little extra time, too. If you're going to be serious about being successful with this one, you must learn to speak entire words and sentences.

For example, "Love ya, Hon" doesn't qualify as a word "touch." It's acceptable for your dog or your guppy, but it's not going to work with your daughter. If you want to tell her you love her, say "I love you." Then to seal it, say her name: "I love you, Sandra." "I love you, Jessica." "I love you, Karen."

> *The only way that word "touchings" work is if you have your daughter's undivided attention and you carefully speak each word.*

Don't say it on the fly. Don't say "I love you" when you're trying to juggle your briefcase, a cup of coffee, your jacket, and a bagel on your way out in the morning. Actually, you *can* do it, but it won't count. "I love you" is probably better than "Clean the garage, Jennifer" or "Don't pull the cat's tail, Allison," but it will score you no points.

The only way that word "touchings" work is if you have your daughter's undivided attention and you carefully speak each word.

If you have lots of children, you must take time to speak verbal affection to each one individually. Group "touchings" are nice, but they, too, don't count for much. If you have a lot of kids and you try to single out one of them with a word "touching," you know how difficult it is to hit the right name first. If you've cleverly titled all your children with names beginning with the same letter, you're getting what you deserve.

Sing and Scratch

No, the heading above does not refer to what many baseball players do during the singing of the national anthem. If you really want to have some fun with your girl, look for opportunities to *combine* verbal and physical touchings. There may be no better time for this than bedtime.

Picture sitting on the edge of the bed. Your daughter is lying on her stomach, and you're rubbing her back. While you're doing that, you are speaking words like this: "You know, Susan, I was talking to some of my friends at work today. I was telling them about how proud I am of you. As I was driving home, I got to thinking that if I could pick a daughter from all the girls who have ever lived, I would pick you first."

Because my wife has a pretty singing voice, her verbal and physical duo included some songs along with the back-scratching. The girls called it "Sing and Scratch." It became an often-requested way to end our daughters' day. Think of it, multisensory affection poured out on little girls, sealing their knowledge of their parent's love for them.

There are several important "do nots" to follow concerning verbal affection. Maybe these will be helpful to you:

Do not exaggerate

When you speak kind words to your girl, don't say things you both know are untrue. If you say, "You're the smartest girl in the whole world," your daughter will know, based on the experience of that day at school, that this is not true. It won't count. Don't even say, "You're the prettiest girl in the world." For the moment, that may be affirming to her, but in time, she'll realize it's not true. One visit to the magazines at the grocery checkout will negate this one.

Instead, talk about your love for her. Say kind things that speak to your appreciation for her thoughtfulness or character.

Don't compliment other girls on things your daughter will never achieve.

Let's say that you and your family are at your favorite restaurant. And let's say that another family comes into the restaurant, walking past you on the way to their table. Let's also say they have a girl who looks to be about the age of your daughter. And let's say that you utter something like, "Wow, look at that little girl's beautiful, curly, blonde hair."

Your daughter is sitting there with straight, mouse-brown hair. And until she's old enough to drive herself to a beauty salon, she's never going to have curly, blonde hair. (Actually, I wonder how many girls fix their hair to please their dads who always said nice things about other girls' hair.)

Or you might say, "Look how tall and slender that little girl is. I'll bet she's going to be a basketball player."

Instead of "hearing" something nice about another girl, your daughter will quickly realize she doesn't measure up. God didn't give her skinny legs and a tall physique. So she may stop eating, trying to please you by becoming something—or someone—she'll never be.

When you compliment her, don't add anything. Just stick to the issue.

As she's walking off the soccer field after a sound performance, simply tell your girl she did a good job. Don't add comments about how bad the other team was or how unfair the referee was. Don't tell her you love her because she did a good job. And remember, don't tell her she's a world-class soccer player. It doesn't count if you do.

If she helps with the dishes after a meal, thank her for being so thoughtful, and leave it at that. Don't say anything about how you used to help your mother before the age of dishwashers or how you helped with the laundry down at the riverbank. Just thank her for her helpfulness. If you tell her she's the most thoughtful girl in the world, you'll need to keep her from finding out about Mother Teresa.

Affection and Boys

As your daughter grows, you'll notice that she's noticing boys. You'll hear her talking about that "hot" boy over there. The first time you hear her talking like that, you might get a little nervous. Thoughts of such a boy (monster) taking a liking to your girl, then attempting some form of affection on her, may make you feel nauseated.

As she turns 16 and begins to single date, you'll see her walking to a boy's car and holding his hand. You'll see her sitting close to him in the front seat. You'll probably feel sad or afraid.

Relax. Your "hedge" around her has been built with *your* loving touch and tender words. If a girl goes out with a boy and her dad has *neglected* these things, then her need for physical affection will not have been satisfied. She'll be looking for love, as the song warns, in all the wrong places.

Fill her heart with a dad's love so that when she encounters a man with less nobility and virtue (and more active hormones), she won't be vulnerable to his advances. And because you've taught her how to talk to you, she'll tell you what happened out there. When the secrecy is taken away, your fear will subside.

Teaching her the art of conversation will also protect her physically with boys. Your girl will have the confidence and skill to say, "I'm sorry, that's unacceptable," rather than quietly acquiesce to his advances. And remember, "making out" usually begins when talking stops.

Daddy, Hold Me

I have a close friend who, after 13 years of marriage, was facing a painful divorce. His days were filled with lawyer meetings and the inevitable hassle of deciding what stuff was whose.

Right in the middle of this turmoil, his six-year-old daughter began to have wetting-her-pants accidents. They started at night, but eventually they happened at all times of the day.

My frustrated friend challenged his girl's "unacceptable" behavior. He tried everything he could—punishment, rewards, books, and experts on the subject—but to no avail.

Finally, after he had had enough of this foolishness, he picked up his girl in his arms, walked to an overstuffed chair in the living room, and sat down. With all he was going through, a defiant little girl was the last thing he needed.

He held her in his arms for a few quiet minutes, then broke the silence with a question. "Do you know how frustrated I am with you, Carrie?" he began. "I've tried everything to get you to stop wetting your pants, but you just continue."

Carrie began crying but said nothing.

"You're six years old. It's been a long time since you learned how to use the bathroom." His anger and disappointment were clearly showing through his words. "Carrie, you're a big girl. Big girls don't wet their pants. *Babies* wet their pants."

Without looking at him, Carrie sat there, cuddled in her father's arms. She finally said, "Yes, and daddies *hold* their babies, don't they?"

His daughter's words found my friend's heart like a laser-guided missile. He had been so absorbed in picking up the pieces of his broken family that he had forgotten to hold his little girl.

Keeping a Healthy Balance in Your Account

In his best-selling book *His Needs, Her Needs,* Dr. Willard Harley offers the helpful concept of deposits and withdrawals in relationships. He talks about how, when good and kind things are done in a relationship, "deposits" are made in that person's "Love Bank" account. When hurtful or potentially threatening things happen, "withdrawals" are made.

Taking time to pour affection on your daughter will not only bring her a great deal of joy, but it will also pave the way for you to help build and shape her character. She'll give you "permission" to be tough (withdrawals) when she knows you've been tender (deposits).

The next chapter deals with correction and discipline. However, if you haven't made plenty of physical and verbal affection deposits in your account at your daughter's love bank, you'll overdraw. Your disciplining check will bounce.

Insufficient funds.

Don't Forget to Love Her Mother

In late October 1974, our second daughter was born. We had been told that the second birth is always easier than the first. Be careful of people who tell you such things; they may lie about other things as well.

When our first daughter was born, we—mostly Bobbie—spent $14\frac{1}{2}$ hours in labor. But when Julie was born, it was almost 18 hours. The reason was that instead of being born headfirst, she was in the breech position—head up. We had gone through all the predelivery classes, earning me a ticket to the delivery room, but because of the complications, when Bobbie was wheeled in, I had to wait in the hallway outside.

In about an hour, the doctor emerged from the operating room with two messages: You have a little girl, and there's "something wrong with her leg."

Although we've never gotten a conclusive diagnosis on Julie's leg, in those first few years of her life, we met with dozens of specialists and made many trips to hospitals all around the Chicago area. The trauma of this on a young couple was unbelievable. The professional warnings that Julie might never walk were difficult to handle, especially for me.

Then, right in the middle of all this, I got a card from a close friend, several years my senior. After a few encouraging sentences, he wrote something I'll never forget. My wise friend said, "Don't forget that the most important thing you can do to be the dad Julie is going to need is to never stop loving her mother."

The words hit me like a straight left. Somehow, in the middle of all this uncertainty and pain, I had forgotten to keep my love for Bobbie on the front burner. I will always be grateful for the gift of those words.

And to you I pass on the same wisdom. As you learn how to demonstrate love to your daughter, don't forget that loving her mother is even more important. Through your open affection for your wife, your daughter will catch a firsthand glimpse of what it's like to be in a loving relationship with a man. It will help to guide her as she looks for the man who will someday be her husband. It will provide a model that she'll be able to reproduce . . . because she will know exactly what it looks like.

Demonstrate affection to your daughter. And don't forget to keep loving your wife.

BUILDER'S CHECKLIST

1. *Touch your daughter:* This can be done in small, nondramatic ways, patting her knee as you drive to the store or squeezing her hand during church. Remember that touching your daughter has no age limitations.

2. *Speak affection to your daughter:* Take the time necessary to clearly speak words of affection to your girl. Don't be tempted into thinking you're doing something helpful if you do this on the run.

3. *Recognize that doing generous things is good, but it's not the same as genuine affection:* Because some dads are uncomfortable with some of the material in this book, they may say, "Well, I'll just be extra generous at birthdays and Christmas." That's nice, but that's not going to do the job.

4. *Make plenty of deposits:* Your demonstrations of affection to your daughter will make deposits in your account at her bank. No one is ever concerned about receiving too many deposits.

CHAPTER SIX

Discipline:
A sledgehammer, a couple of crowbars, and a level

"If all our wishes were gratified, most of our pleasures would be destroyed."

RICHARD WHATELY

W e were in a hurry. I hollered upstairs to tell Bobbie that I'd go ahead and pull the car out of the garage. "I'll meet you on the driveway in front of the house," I said.

I didn't wait for her answer.

I crawled into our three-year-old Cutlass, more than a little anxious to get on with it. But when I turned the ignition key, I heard a weird sound. Over the years, "college cars" and all, I've tried to start cars with dead batteries, but this particular noise had escaped me. The best way to describe it was that it was almost human-sounding . . . like a guy with a kidney stone.

In any case, my Oldsmobile was dead. I slid the gearshift to "N" and walked around to the front to push it out of the garage. Aaarrgghhh. Kidney stones can be very heavy. Fortunately, our driveway slopes gently to the street. Once the car had some momentum, I jumped behind the wheel to make sure the position of our mailbox did not get readjusted unintentionally.

After the car was all the way to the street, I walked back to the garage and fired up Julie's car. I backed it down the driveway and parked it face to face with my dead Olds. On my way back to the garage to get my jumper cables, a thought flashed across my mind: *Does Julie know what to do with jumper cables?* As a sophomore in college and with a little car of her own, she probably had never had to jump-start a dead car.

Throughout their process of fathering, dads look for teaching moments. Most of the time, those moments call for something besides a lesson, but most dads push through that nonsense and deliver a memorable—at least to them—lecture nonetheless. This, however, *was* a legitimate teaching moment.

In a few minutes, Julie was standing on the street with me. I had the cables in my hands and was explaining that the black clamp goes on the negative battery post and the red goes on the positive. I also observed that battery manufacturers now color-code battery posts— positive is red and negative is black. Modern technology has mercilessly taken one more teaching opportunity from us.

As I stood there explaining how to safely take the charge from the good battery and use it to start the dead car, Julie interrupted me with a question. "Dad," she queried, "do you know *why* a battery has a positive and a negative?"

I took a long, deep breath, preparing my answer. (I also wasn't sure if this was a real question or if I was being set up by my science-and-math-loving 20-year-old.)

I took another breath.

"They have a positive and a negative because in order to make anything work right, you *need* both a positive and a negative," I finally said, thinking a little enthusiasm might lead her to believe this was an actual answer.

Julie smiled at me, knowing I had just tried to bluff her and didn't get away with it. I smiled back, realizing that with two years of physics behind her, she knew full well why a battery has a positive and a negative. I used to know, but I forgot. She dropped the subject.

I went on with the "jumper cable lesson."

Regardless, the principle is correct. To make things work, there must be a positive and a negative. Both are necessary.

In the last chapter, we talked a lot about the positive—touching, squeezing, hugging, writing, and speaking tender words. As a dad, you must do those things. But if you had stopped reading at the end of that chapter and skipped this one, you'd be in deep weeds. Better said, your *daughter* would be in trouble.

There must be a positive side and a negative side to your relationship with her.

How much positive and how much negative? Please hear me on this: *100 percent* positive and *100 percent* negative. Crank them both up the whole way. Be the most affirming and tender dad you've ever heard of, *and* be the most no-nonsense, strict father on the planet. Under any conditions, please do not try to be one without the other.

> *Be the most affirming and tender dad you've ever heard of,* and *be the most no-nonsense, strict father on the planet.*

Using the Right Tools

When I'm about to frame a room with two-by-fours, two-by-sixes, and such, I always have three tools close by: a 16-pound sledgehammer, a crowbar, and a four-foot level.

My job is to make sure every wall is perfectly vertical—the bubble on the level is *squarely* in the middle on every one. Why? Because I also enjoy hanging wallpaper, and if the internal structure of the walls isn't right, wallpapering—especially with striped wallpaper—is no fun at all.

Unfortunately, the sledge and the crowbar are noisy to use. And though I prefer listening to a Chopin concerto to hearing the loud noises these tools make, I'm willing to endure that temporary discomfort in exchange for walls that are straight and true.

Discipline—the Noun and the Verb

The word *discipline* can be either a noun or a verb, depending on how it's used. The goal is to "build" a daughter who's a disciplined person—a woman who is able to exercise self-control; a woman whose interior structure is straight and true; a woman who knows personal discipline. That's *discipline* the noun. It's what you're shooting for.

And how do you get there? *Discipline* the verb. An athlete achieves discipline—noun—by submitting himself to the discipline—verb—of his coach or trainer. The joy and pleasure—positive—of being a disciplined person—noun—makes the pain—negative—of disciplining—verb—a worthwhile investment. Whew!

Lots of Raw Material

When your daughter is born, she has no discipline. None. If she's hungry, she cries. If she has to go, she goes. When all these things are taken care of and she still wants to make your life miserable, she may still feel like crying, so she does. When she's sleepy, she sleeps. And when she wakes up again and wants any of the above, she'll cry again. She has no ability to rein herself in.

You, on the other hand, have discipline. Most of the time, you understand self-talk and restraint. You may feel like going absolutely berserk at some guy on the freeway who decides to cut you off, but you . . . er . . . uh . . . bad example. Anyway, for the most part, you live a disciplined life.

You may not feel like getting out of bed for work, but you do it anyway. You may not enjoy exercise, keeping your garage in order, using deodorant every day, or saying "good morning" to the office receptionist, but you've learned to count on yourself to do those things. On a self-discipline scale of 1 to 10, let's say you're an 8.

Your job with your little zero is to get her to an eight, where you are, or higher if you've married well. How do you do this? Through *discipline* the verb: setting guidelines and inspecting results. How long do you do this? Until her discipline—noun—kicks into auto pilot.

In our culture, this is a controversial issue. Spanking is called "hitting." Verbal correction is referred to as "emotional abuse." In fact, this chapter may get me in a lot of trouble, but I'm willing to face it head on. (By the way, we're moving and don't have the new phone number yet. I'll get that to you as soon as I can.)

Warning: The next several pages must be read by a disciplined person. In the wrong hands, this information will be like dynamite—explosive and very dangerous. In the right hands, it will be like a spark plug to gasoline vapor: explosive but accelerating your daughter forward.

Guidelines for Disciplining

To be a successful disciplinarian, you need to follow four extremely important guidelines. Remember that you don't discipline because you enjoy it. In fact, if doing it gives you pleasure, stop and get some help for yourself.

The reason you discipline is that you're making an investment in your daughter. You're exercising your own discipline—consistently doing the right thing even if you don't feel like it—in creating discipline in your daughter.

Here are the guidelines you need to observe:

Rules must be clearly defined and consistently enforced

How would you like to play baseball if only the umpires knew where the foul lines were? And what if they changed from inning to inning? You'd be circling the bases, thinking you just hit a home run, but the umpire might tell you that in the *third* inning that would have been a round-tripper, but this is the *sixth* inning, and now it's an automatic out.

You trudge into the dugout and plop down on the bench, disliking the umpire and probably the whole stupid game as well.

Set guidelines for your daughter: toys back in the box when she's finished playing; finish her vegetables before enjoying dessert; no running in the living room; in bed by 9:00; no disrespectful back-talking allowed; and so on. Be sure she clearly understands. Don't make these up as you go. If you do, no punishment should be given on the first infraction.

Then be consistent with rules and the penalties when they're deliberately broken. Never, ever punish for honest mistakes. Dads who punish for spilled milk ought to caned in the office cafeteria during lunch.

Discipline must be swift

The effectiveness of your discipline will depend on the amount of time between the infraction and the corresponding correction—the less time the more effective; the more time the less effective.

Several years ago, a fad swept the country. It encouraged parents to count to three prior to expecting their child to obey.

I can envision these people in the grocery store. Their son is walking toward a man-sized pyramid of green beans on special. He's got total annihilation of the merchandise in mind, and his mother tells him, "You come back here right now, Sheldon."

Sheldon pauses, glancing over his right shoulder to see if the voice is his mother's and, if it is, whether she's actually addressing him. Nice try, Sheldon.

He turns back toward Del Monte Mountain, accelerating his pace.

"Sheldon, I said you come back here," pleads his mother. Then, almost robotlike, she begins to count: "One, twooooo . . . "

Watching this bizarre scene, I'm taken back to all-neighborhood, all-evening kick-the-can marathons. I can see the kid who's "it" standing with his face against the coarse bark of the huge elm tree in our front yard, his hands cupped around the outside of his eyes, counting. The mother in the grocery store reminds me of one of those youngsters counting—neither one of them is seeing very clearly.

Don't count.

The guideline for your daughter is this: When your dad—or your mother—asks you to obey, you obey. When do you obey? The first time you're asked.

Our girls knew about this so well that when they hesitated, we would say, "When do you obey?" And they would respond, "The first time." ("The foost tahm," before they could enunciate well.)

You're going to find this guideline extremely inconvenient. Why? Because you and I are, by nature, lazy. We would rather delay the consequence of our daughter's misbehavior until a more convenient time: "Go to your room until this game gets to halftime; *then* we'll deal with your lack of self-control."

Discipline must be painful

Go with me, right now, on a little mental journey to your favorite state penitentiary. We're going to walk up and down the cell blocks conducting brief interviews with the various inmates. We're going to ask them if this is what they had in mind when they were kids. We'll ask them if they're happy. Fulfilled. Living the life they had dreamed about.

Or are they in pain?

There may be nothing as awful—painful—as living an undisciplined life and not being able to go back and fix it. People waste their lives, sitting in a 9 by 12 in Leavenworth, having acted spontaneously. For one moment in time, they did what came naturally, and now they're sitting out life.

In his best-selling book *The Road Less Traveled,* M. Scott Peck called life "hard." He was right. And an undisciplined life is even harder and more painful.

Just below my left shoulder, at the top of my arm, is a dime-sized scar. A doctor gave me that scar when I was seven. All I remember about getting my smallpox vaccination was that he used two needles to inflict this terrible thing on me.

In the past few years, I've learned what a smallpox vaccination really is. It's literally . . . smallpox. Of course, it's administered safely, under sound medical conditions, but it's actually smallpox—a little dose of *the real thing*.

Now, follow me on this one: If living out an undisciplined life is an extremely unpleasant and painful experience, then disciplining a person toward self-discipline should mean small doses of the real thing—painful inflictions under sound and loving family conditions.

And what constitutes "painful" discipline?

For starters, it's *not* words.

Imagine that you were speeding along a lonesome country road, oblivious to the speed limit. Suddenly, in the distance, you see a person—he looks a lot like a policeman—standing on the shoulder. After you fly past him, you see him in your rearview mirror, scream-ing at you. Of course, traveling at mach one, you can't actually hear anything. But you can tell he's really into it, because he's jumping up and down and shaking his fists.

Do you slow down? Not unless you've inadvertently eased up on the accelerator while watching the officer dance.

Unfortunately—and this is from personal experience—that's not what really happens. Policemen understand the "value" of swift (do not try to outrun that benign-looking car with the blackwalls and the lights on top) and painful (what else could you have done with that $150 dollars?) action as a direct result of your intentional (you saw the signs) disobedience.

For your daughter, "painful" discipline may be a spanking. Or it may be taking away a privilege. But for it to be effective, it must provide enough discomfort that she says to herself, *You know, that wasn't fun. I think I'll do whatever I can to avoid that in the future.* Mission accomplished.

Discipline must be fair

The Old Testament calls it "an eye for an eye and a tooth for a tooth." And, until recently, I had no idea what that really meant.

Actually, it's a simple principle: Jewish law provided that if you stole a man's mule, you had to replace it. If you burned a man's barn down, you were responsible to rebuild it. If you took someone's life, you should pay with your own.

"Fairness" in disciplining means that the punishment should match the "crime." If your daughter leaves a mess, make her clean it up. Don't spank her. If she hurts her friend, walk her to her friend's house, and make her ask for forgiveness. Don't spank her. If she blatantly disobeys you or speaks disrespectfully to you, spank her.

Remember that you're giving her a little dose of the real thing.

A spanking when she's six *is not as painful* as a lost job or broken marriage when she's 28 because you didn't teach her how to control her tongue. She might not understand this when she's six, but swift, painful, and fair punishment is one of the most important "gifts" you'll ever give your daughter.

Time Out for Some Perspective

You can be sure that some folks will take *swift* and *painful* and say this book advocates hauling off and blasting your daughter the moment she steps out of line. *No, no, no.* I'm not advocating that. I despise that kind of punishment. It's often filled with rage, and the one being disciplined usually walks away more angry at the one who delivered the correction than she is at herself for the infraction.

Mission *not* accomplished.

Take a moment, once your daughter has disobeyed—or whatever—to calm down. Talk to her about what she did and why you believe it deserves punishment. Actually, you won't be as likely to be enraged if you act swiftly, as the girls said, "the first time." If you act right away, you'll have more of your own composure intact. If, on the other hand, you've been sitting there, watching repeated infractions and "complaining" about them to your daughter, you may be more likely to explode in frustration and anger.

Regardless, take a deep breath. You're teaching her something; you're not blowing off steam or getting even.

Along those lines, here are a few hints:

No yelling

Yes, during a punishment, your voice is going to be more intense than when you ask for the salt to be passed at the dinner table, but no yelling allowed. Angry outbursts are *never* productive. Yelling does not inflict the right kind of pain. It will most often direct itself to your daughter's *person* rather than to her *deed.* Flag on the play. If you yell at your daughter, you *must* apologize to her, which doesn't do much for the lesson *she's* supposed to be learning.

Spank under control

My wife and I spanked about 15 times. That is, we held the girls over our knee and paddled 15 times with our hand. Your hand will be an adequate "pain" gauge, helping you not to forget that some serious discomfort is going on here. We didn't spank hard. It was the repetition that communicated the message. This was not an angry swat;

this was a "spanking." There's a big difference. If you hit your daughter in anger, you *must* apologize to her, which doesn't do much for the lesson *she's* supposed to be learning.

Some experts, including Dr. James Dobson, recommend using a neutral object—a ruler, wooden spoon, or hair brush—for spanking. In their professional opinion, this object represents a more distant instrument than their parent's hand—something that should be reserved for holding and loving your child. (See Dr. Dobson's book *The New Dare to Discipline*, p. 64.) But our experience was that our hand, like the car battery with positive and negative poles, was the proper instrument for both—that physical punishment was as intimate and personal as physical tenderness.

Spanking was not something we did *to* our daughters. It was a shared and painful experience, acknowledging that there had been a breech in our relationship that must be bridged—a "foreign object" that must be excised. It wasn't a happy moment in our relationship, but, ultimately, it became a building block, as important between us as our occasional visits to the frozen yogurt shop.

Always punish privately

If you embarrass your daughter, shame on *you*. Like yelling, creating embarrassment focuses pain on the wrong thing. If you're in

> *If you embarrass your daughter, shame on* you.

public and she has just done something punishable, try to catch her eye. Let her know you saw what she did and you're not pleased. She'll get the message. Even if you take her to another room to punish her, your dramatic whisking of her from a public place creates an unnecessary, embarrassing event.

Disciplining your daughter is an intimate and secret thing. Don't do it in public. Don't let your daughter catch you telling your friends —or, worse, *her* friends—about it, either. If you embarrass your daughter, you *must* apologize to her, which doesn't do much for the lesson *she's* supposed to be learning.

Something Magic Inside?

Many years ago, while it was still in black and white, I saw an episode of "Candid Camera." The producers had placed a gyroscope—the kind used in aircraft and space-travel navigation—inside a suitcase. Then, posing as a hotel guest, Alan Funt asked the bellman to take his bag to his room.

The unsuspecting bellman happily agreed, picked up the heavy bag, and walked toward the elevators. As he reached them, he turned to enter the first open lift, but the suitcase "wouldn't" turn. It had, as my mother used to say, "a mind of its own."

The bellman was astonished. He had never carried a bag that didn't follow his carry. Even the thought of such a thing had never entered his mind.

It was a funny scene, all right, but the message was unforgettable. Creating the gyroscope—her own ability to make good choices in spite of outside pressure—inside your daughter can begin when she's quite young.

Say No Once a Day

This may sound a bit extreme, but when our girls were young, we experimented with self-discipline. We created a game called "Did you say no to yourself today?" We challenged everyone around the supper table to "say no to yourself at least one time tomorrow, and then report your story at the next evening's supper."

It doesn't have to be a bad thing we're saying no to, just something like turning the television off a half hour before we really want to or limiting our after-school snack to one cookie instead of two.

At dinner time the following evening, we talked about how well we did. We made it fun, but the results of doing this created the ability, for all of us, to keep ourselves in check. Discipline, the noun.

Reports the next day were things like the following.

Dad's report: "At lunch today, I was about to order a slice of pie for dessert, but I decided that since I had a dessert yesterday, I'd say no today. So I said no."

Everyone cheered Dad's good report . . . not necessarily because he was getting a little fat and needed to go on a diet, but because he was able to tell himself no and make it stick.

Teenage daughter's report: "I was on the phone with my best friend. I had some homework that needed to be finished, so I told her I could only talk for five more minutes. In a little while, I glanced back at the clock and realized my time was up. Even though I *really* wanted to keep talking, I told my friend that I had work to do and hung up."

The whole family celebrated, not because the phone was overly tied up but because our daughter made a rule and then obeyed it, all on her own.

Little girl's report: "My friend offered me some leftover Halloween candy right before dinner, and I said, 'No, thank you.'"

Again, the family cheered our daughter's ability to make a good decision all by herself.

We were learning together, before being faced with life-and-death situations, to fine-tune our own self-imposed navigation system.

Your job, as the father of a girl, is to use externally imposed disciplining through punishments or even through playing the "no" game, and to create the internal discipline—the gyroscope—that gives her a will of her own.

There will come a day when your daughter is making every

decision—big and small—without your direct influence. What you want is for her to make good choices simply because they're good choices, not because her dad will be there to make sure they're good choices!

God's Idea of a Good Time

At the very moment I'm writing this, I'm looking out on a mid-October Tennessee morning. The sky is crystal clear, the bluest blue you could ever imagine. Because we've had lots of rain, our yard is a spectacular shade of green. The leaves of the trees in the woods behind our house are just beginning to give us a hint of the vibrant fall colors to come.

But, as hard as it may be for me to imagine, the Garden of Eden makes the scene out my window look like a smoldering city dump.

Not only was Eden pretty to look at, but it was also "perfect" in every way. Man's relationship to woman was flawless. Woman's relationship to man was without dissension or fear. And both of their relationships with their Creator were impeccable. Adam and Eve were delighted at all of this.

Amazingly, right in the middle of this pristine flawlessness was a "no"—an exquisite tree whose fruit couldn't be eaten. Isn't that amazing? The Garden of Eden included a "no."

Most of the time, I think of enjoyment as meaning "no boundaries." No inhibitions. No "no's," if you will. All "yeses." But like the battery in my dead Oldsmobile, in order to work right, life must include the positive *and* the negative.

Ralph Foote

When I was a senior in college, I found myself pushing the edges a little on conduct. I guess my parents' teaching and admonitions were somewhere between planting and harvest in my heart, if you know what I mean.

Because of that, I often stayed out late. I don't mean late, I mean *late*. And sometimes, in returning to campus, I'd see a young man running along the country roads that surrounded our school. Here it was, the middle of the night, and this person was running all by himself.

I found out that the runner was a sophomore from a small Indiana town. His name was Ralph Foote, and he was a serious runner. I'm not exactly sure how often I saw Ralph on his midnight runs; I only know that it was many, many times.

I remember thinking, *Poor Ralph. College life certainly isn't as much fun for him as it is for me. Why doesn't he stop all this running and begin to enjoy himself? Hey, you only go around once.*

The following spring, I learned that the track coach was looking for some help for the conference track meet. Taylor University was hosting the event, and there was a need for timers and helpers to move hurdles, rake the sand in the broad jump pit, set the bars for the high jump and pole vault, and so forth. I volunteered.

Near the end of the afternoon, the announcer called the runners to the starting line for the two-mile run. Having been a wanna-be distance runner in junior high, I had always been impressed by those who had the guts to run the long ones. And, since I didn't have any current assignments for other events, I crawled up to the top of the press tower to watch.

When the gun sounded, the mass of runners took off like a single, multiheaded creature. But by the end of the second lap, the creature had substantially thinned out. Several men — maybe six or seven — were leading, the rest of the field stretching out for 30 yards.

By the time the runners finished the first mile, the distance between the guys in front and those in the back was the length of the straightaway—almost a full half lap. The lead pack was down to three.

This running triplet hung together for three laps. Step for step, they were pacing each other with gliding and synchronized strides. As the timers in the press box glanced at their watches, the excitement began to build. "There could be a new conference record set in the two mile," I overheard them say. Maybe a new *state* record.

In distance races, the starter fires the gun when the first runner begins his last lap. This is cleverly referred to as the "gun lap." When the gun sounded, announcing that this running triumvirate had crossed the starting line for the last time, something unbelievable happened. As I write these words, almost 30 years later, I feel the overwhelming emotion of what I saw that day as though I'm experiencing it for the first time.

Before the sound of the shot had finished reverberating through the woods behind the track, a single runner seemed to explode from the pack of three. As though propelled by a slingshot, he took off in a dead sprint. And, although the other two runners had picked up their own pace a bit, it looked as though they had come to a complete stop.

The entire stadium came to its feet. Field-event competitors finishing their efforts stood frozen. The lead runner, a sophomore named Ralph Foote, had been waiting for this moment. The faithful discipline of late-night running on those lonely Indiana country roads was seeking its rightful reward.

For a full quarter mile, Ralph did not slow his pace. The dead sprint he began at the start of the gun lap did not slack.

By the time Ralph rounded the last turn for the final dash to the tape, every person in the stadium was screaming his support for this 19-year-old. Even the athletes and coaches from other schools were cheering him on.

When the time was posted, Ralph Foote had scraped a full 11

seconds off the school record in the two mile, and more than 10 seconds off the conference record. (The spring before, he had broken the previous conference record by 19.3 seconds! And just for good measure, Ralph set still another new record—this time the state mark—in the two mile a year later.)

I have a question: Who was the happiest man in the stadium that Saturday afternoon?

Correct. It was Ralph Foote.

Why? Because he had turned the disciplining and grueling pain of faithful training into the rewards of being the most disciplined two-miler in the history of the school. And the conference. And the state.

Discipline is its *own* reward.

Your assignment is to brand an image of your daughter as a happy, balanced, disciplined, and complete woman in your mind. Then, create a system of swift, painful, and fair disciplines that successfully get her to that destination.

Your job is not to be *liked*. Your job is to be *faithful* and *effective*. If you're doing the right things, there will be days when you'll come in dead last in the "Dad of the Year Sweepstakes." That's okay. Don't give up. Hang in there. This one's especially tough for quitters like us. But you can do it.

Does this sound like a lot of gut-wrenching work? Well, there *are* days when it's not that easy, but, trust me, the whole process can be a lot of fun, too. We're going to talk about that next.

BUILDER'S CHECKLIST

1. *Remember the "good life" is both positive and negative:* Although we tend to believe that positive is always good and negative is always bad, only a few things that are truly worthwhile do not include both.

2. *Think of discipline as both a verb and a noun:* To help your daughter reach the goal of internal self-discipline, it's necessary to impose external disciplining.

3. *Make punishment swift, painful, and fair:* Waiting too long between the infraction and the penalty diminishes the impact of the punishment. A consequence that isn't painful is not a consequence at all; it's simply a slight inconvenience. And when the sentence doesn't match the severity of the crime, it will be seen as unfair and will lose its impact.

4. *Be sure your life matches your words:* If you intend to be the disciplinarian, you'd better be prepared to make your words match your own life.

5. *Teach that discipline is its own reward:* The achievement of personal discipline can be a great thrill all by itself. It doesn't even have to "accomplish" anything useful to have significant value.

Laughter:
Did you hear the one about…?

"Laughter is the shortest distance between two people."

VICTOR BORGE

In March 1982, I received a letter that changed my life. At least, that's what it said it was going to do.

The outside of the envelope promised that "You Have Already Won." The letter inside explained the details. My name had been "specially drawn" from a list of millions, and, of the eight wonderful awards listed, I *had won* one of the prizes with a check mark next to it. Here was the checked list:

A Jeep Cherokee:	I love Jeeps. I've always wanted one.
A boat:	Water skiing is one of my favorite sports.
A Weed-Eater:	That's probably the one I really won, because it's the cheapest, but hey, my lawn could use a Weed-Eater.
A big-screen TV:	Now you're talking: the Chicago Bears— life-size!

All we had to do to claim our prize was drive to Fort Worth— about a hundred miles away—and listen to a "brief, two-hour presentation." And although the girls were skeptical, I was able to talk them into making the trip with some subtle salesmanship:

"If we win the television, I'll let you stay up every night as long as you want for the rest of your life. You can watch any show, and I'll never tell you to turn it off."

"If we win the Jeep, I'll let you drive. So what if you're only 11 and eight! Silly rules like having a driver's license aren't really necessary.

Plus, I have some lawyer friends."

"If we win the Weed-Eater, I'll cut your grass when you get married and have a house of your own."

"If we win the boat . . ."

As I said, they agreed to take the trip to Fort Worth.

When we arrived at "Lake Awesome & Spectacular Estates & Country Club," I remember being impressed with the massive brick-and-stone entrance. It was the size of Wrigley Field, complete with more-meticulous landscaping than the entrance to Busch Gardens. Unfortunately, that was all there was. No permanent buildings. No golf course. Come to think of it, no lake, either. Just the huge entrance nicely paved and curbed, with underground utilities, roads leading to more nicely paved roads, also with curbs and under-ground utilities.

There were also several double-wide trailers just inside the entrance, where we had the rare opportunity of meeting Nick, our friendly and talkative salesman. My guess was that Nick had been given the choice of two years down the river, 500 hours of commu-nity service, or this.

As he got deeper and deeper into his presentation, I could see that I was losing my family. Whenever I caught their eyes, they'd give me this "Please-please-get-me-out-of-here-or-I'll-die" look. So I quickly fixed that problem.

I stopped looking at them.

Exactly two hours later, Nick was finished—more finished than he ever knew. He asked if we were interested in purchasing a lot at "Lake Awesome & Spectacular," and, after what I thought was enough time of "seriously thinking about it," I told him I thought we'd need to put that decision on hold. *Yeah, like on hold till the glaciers make it to Fort Worth.*

Then, acting very disappointed at our decision to pass on this once-in-a-lifetime opportunity, he asked to see our letter, the one promising the prize. I gladly handed it over. As he scanned the list of "awards we had won," I looked at my family with that air of confident assurance. I was thinking, *This'll be worth it all, girls. In just a few moments, you'll forget the past two hours of torture. You'll be happy, and I'll be a hero.*

After acting as if he were checking the code number on our letter against the master notebook of code numbers, Nick stroked his chin, gave a little "hmmm" sound, and raised his eyebrows to indicate he really regretted having to part with such a valuable thing. "It looks like you've won the boat," he finally announced.

The girls squealed with delight. "A boat! Wow, Dad, a boat!"

Oh, no, I recall thinking, *I don't have a trailer hitch on my car.* This is the truth. That thought *really* crossed my mind.

Nick excused himself to go "get the boat," and we walked outside to the front of the double-wide, where my hitchless car was parked. The girls asked if I thought we might be able to put the boat into a lake near our home soon. I assured them we'd do that just as soon as possible.

In a few minutes, Nick appeared with the boat . . . in his hand. It was the inflate-to-25-pounds, made-in-the-Proud-and-Sovereign-Republic-of-Barbados "Sea Cloud Sport Boat." *"Warning: Not to be used as a life preserver"* was printed on the side of the clear plastic bag he proudly handed me.

The girls gasped, but before they could actually say anything, I had them corralled into the car, and we were off, driving back through — for the last time ever — the massive brick-and-stone entrance.

Good bye, "Lake Whatever & Who Cares Estates."

The drive back to our home was not pleasant. I apologized for being so stupid and gullible. I apologized again. I promised that when I died, all my estate would be split between the two girls and that, even if we had more kids, the new ones, because they hadn't been forced to endure Nick, wouldn't get a dime.

We stopped for sundaes.

Be Happy

The story of the Sea Cloud Sport Boat has provided our family with more value than any 16-foot, fiberglass sloop ever could have. I've told the story countless times. The girls have brought friends home and said, "Dad, tell Audrey the story of the Sea Cloud Sport Boat." And we've laughed again.

In the Gospels, Jesus opened the Sermon on the Mount—His magnum opus sermon—with a description of what it takes to be "happy." It's almost as though He were saying, "You'll know you've arrived in My kingdom when your life is marked with happiness."

Several years ago, Bobbie and I were visiting a large church in Southern California. The pastor is our friend, and he has a wonderful ability to laugh. He does it all the time, even in the middle of his sermons.

After the service, we bumped into a man we hadn't seen for many years. He had moved to California from Chicago, where we had last seen him, to be the dean of a small, denominational, Christian college. Because his particular denomination and the one represented by the church we were standing in were very different, I was surprised to see him.

"What are *you* doing here?" I asked, making no attempt to hide my surprise.

"Well, I *know* my Christian tradition is very different from this one," he replied. "But I love the minister here. He doesn't take himself too seriously."

What an interesting distinction, I reflected later. *Of all the profound things he could have said—"I like his teaching" or "I appreciate his crisp delivery" or "I admire his brilliant argumentation"—he enjoys the minister's sense of humor.*

Pretty profound, don't you think?

Be Fun to Live With

Laugh with your girl. Be silly. Fill your home with joy. Buy a pair of Groucho Marx glasses, and come to dinner wearing them. Walk into the room with your arms outstretched, growling like a grizzly bear, and "attack" your girl, tousling her hair and tick-ling her. Do be careful, because you're much bigger and stronger. However, if your wife isn't saying, "Honey, be careful," you're not doing it right! You're not acting "grizzly" enough.

> *Laugh with your girl. Be silly. Fill your home with joy.*

Once I had one of my daughters on the floor, I'd nuzzle my face into the soft skin of her neck and blow out, mak-ing a loud "ZZZrrrrbbbttt." She would squeal. Her mother would call from the other room, "Hey, what are you doing in there?"

"Nothing," I'd reply innocently.

We'd look at each other and giggle knowingly.

Pretty Funny Stuff

Go to a bookstore and buy a riddle book. Okay, so they're a little corny, but your girl will love them. Here are a few examples. Remem-ber these are for you to use with your daughter, so there's no need to smile yourself.

Which side of a chicken has the most feathers?
The outside.

Where do sheep get their hair cut?

At the baa-baa shop.

Why don't ducks tell jokes when they're flying?

They might quack up.

What do you call a cow who works for a gardener?

A lawn moo-er.

Why are fish so smart?

Because they live in schools.

(I put this one in so you'd at least get one right.)

How do baby birds learn to fly?

They wing it.

Why do bees hum?

Because they can't remember the words.

What kind of coat won't keep you warm?

A coat of paint.

When is a door not a door?

When it is ajar.

What's worse than a centipede with sore feet?

A giraffe with a sore throat or a turtle with claustrophobia.

Why is honey so scarce in Boston?

Because there's only one "B" in Boston.

What did the beaver say to the tree?

It's been nice gnawing you.

Buy other fun books. One of our favorites was *Hand, Hand, Fingers, Thumb.* I would read the book to the girls and act it out while I was reading: "Millions of fingers, millions of thumbs, millions of monkeys drumming on drums, Dum ditty dum ditty dum dum dum." When we'd get to that last part, one of the girls would "read" along, "Dum ditty dum ditty dum dum dum."

We would laugh.

When the girls got a little older, we bought a video copy of the classic comedy *What's Up, Doc?* with Ryan O'Neil and Barbra Streisand. We watched the video so many times that we—especially the girls—had nearly every line memorized. Then there were times when lines like "Don't shoot me, I'm part Italian" or "Eunice, there's a person named Eunice?" would fit with something we were talking about.

And we would laugh.

Rules for Laughter

Yes, there are rules even for laughter. Unless you follow several guidelines, it could become an unfortunate and hurtful thing.

Laugh *with* your girl, never *at* her

"I was just kidding" rarely fixes a clumsy attempt at person-directed humor. Especially when she's young, you must be careful about the kind of laughter you employ. If it's at your daughter's expense, you'll pay.

Remember that your daughter has a tender and easily breakable heart. You must do your best to protect it.

Find things you can do together that are fun. I've already mentioned funny books and silly movies. But you can add to that list, doing unpredictable and crazy things.

Spontaneity over nutrition

One Friday night, Charles—a serious-minded, CPA-type friend—announced to his daughter, Meg, that he was taking her to breakfast the next morning. She was delighted. Breakfast with Dad was always a lot of fun.

Early the next morning, Charles busied himself with chores around the house, telling his daughter that "in just a little while, we'll be leaving for breakfast." By 10:00, they were off.

"Where are we going for breakfast?" Meg wondered.

"Oh, a special breakfast place" was all Charles would say.

In a few minutes, Charles brought his car to a stop in front of the local Baskin-Robbins. "We're here, Meg," he announced.

"Dad, this is an ice cream place. We don't eat ice cream for breakfast," she said.

"*Today* we do," Charles responded.

In telling me the story, my friend told of his delight in treating his six-year-old to a lavish butterscotch sundae: "Meg was completely shocked by my impulsive, out-of-character morning treat. For weeks she told everybody she saw that her daddy had bought her ice cream for breakfast." And Charles's face told me that the exchange of ice cream for something more nutritious was well worth it.

He also told me he'd had to talk his wife into this one before pulling it off.

Make her laugh.

Laugh at circumstances

Every family has humorous experiences. Ours included the Sea Cloud Sport Boat and many others.

Gary Smalley tells stories of family camping trips. His reason for taking his family on those excursions was that every trip included a crisis: thunderstorms, raccoons, poison ivy . . . the possibilities are endless.

Even if your family isn't into inflatable "ski" boats or camping trips, there are plenty of things you can do together. These activities create the circumstances that naturally produce wonderful, laughable memories.

You can go bowling. You can take long hikes. You can put a jungle gym in your backyard or go to a city park where they have lots of things a dad can do with his daughter: swings, slides, and crawl-through things.

Hint: Always take a camera along. Ask other people if they would please take your picture. As the years go by, these photos of you and your daughter will become visual reminders of those happy times you shared together.

Sometimes the circumstances you laugh at will happen when you're not with your family. Business trips can be a rich source of these stories. Tell your family about them when you get home.

One of my personal favorites was the time I was taking the red-eye flight from Portland to Dallas. When I got to the boarding gate in Portland just before midnight, I asked the gate attendant if he could see if there was a bulkhead seat open. Because of the length of my legs, I like to sit in front of the bulkhead that separates the coach section from first class.

"No, I'm sorry," he said. "There's nothing open on the bulkhead. But if I were you, I'd sit in the exit row. My computer tells me the window seat is open. There's a lot of leg room there."

I don't like to be that far back in the plane, but I told him to go ahead and put me there. Then as an afterthought I said, "Just don't put me next to some 350-pound guy, okay?"

We both laughed.

Twenty minutes later, I boarded the plane. I found my seat and silently thanked the ticket agent for putting me in this roomy space for the long flight to Dallas.

Passengers were making their way down the aisle, finding their seats, then jamming their "carry-on luggage" into the overhead bins. And as I sat there waiting for the plane to fill up, I saw *him* coming. In the distance, just this side of the bulkhead wall, I spotted him. He was the largest man I had ever seen inside an airplane—400 pounds, maybe 450 or 500. As he walked down the aisle, he was so wide that he had to squeeze himself between the seats.

The moment I saw him, I knew, without a shadow of doubt, that his seat assignment was next to me. This was a Super 80, with three seats on one side of the aisle and two on the other. I was in the window seat on the "two" side.

Sure enough, when he got to my row, he turned, stepped into the row in front of the seat next to me, and dropped. I don't mean that he sat down; I mean he lifted his feet off the floor and literally dropped into the seat.

Even with the momentum of his free fall, he was only able to squeeze his way into the first vertical third of his seat. There was no way of checking, but I don't think his wallet ever made it the whole way south to the seat fabric, if you follow my drift. My reason for concluding this was that the top of my head was about even with his shoulder. *This guy's suspended in mid-air,* I thought, *but with the pressure he's exerting on the armrests, he's not going anywhere.*

Once he had taken a seatbelt extension out of his case and buckled up, I took a moment to assess the situation. I realized that what was left of this guy on the port side of his own seat was taking up at least half of my seat space. I was literally trapped between my gargantuan neighbor and the window to my left. I quickly dismissed the chance that I could ever open the computer on my lap. And I seriously doubted I'd be able to get any sleep on this long flight.

Then, to add to the fun, five minutes after we were airborne, the man started to snore. It wasn't the regular, rhythmic kind of snoring my wife accuses me of (although I don't believe her). It actually sounded like a conversation between three or four nervous boars.

I sat there plotting my next move. I knew I had to get out of there. Claustrophobic situations usually have little effect on me, but I felt like a sausage. *Either I get out of here or I start screaming like a nut case,* I resolved.

So, collecting all my strength, I pulled myself out of my seat and across the man's lap to freedom. I thought the whole plane was going to applaud my narrow escape.

I walked to the front of the plane, hoping to find a compassionate flight attendant. But by the time I got to the curtain separating the "have" passengers from the "have-nots," I was depressed. I hadn't spotted even one open seat. At that point I was thinking, *Hey, I'll stand if I have to. Or maybe I could sit this one out in the rest room.*

Pushing my way through the curtain, I saw it. Like a drink of water to a parched desert traveler, I saw it—an open seat. An open *first-class* seat.

When I reached the galley, the flight attendant was busily preparing goodies for her first-class passengers. She looked at me and smiled. *Good,* I thought, *a nice flight attendant.*

"Hi," I said. "I'm sitting in 21A, and—"

"I know who you are," she quickly answered. "I was about to come get you."

"You were?" I responded, unable to hide my surprise.

"Yes," she said. "Unless we move that guy next to you to the window seat, we're not going to be able to get our food cart down the aisle. Why don't you move up here to first class?"

"Oh, I don't know," I countered. "There are so many folks back in coach who are much more deserving than me . . ." (I just made that up.)

No, in a flash I had hustled back to 21A, collected my things, and was enjoying the posh elegance of my new seat. Laying my head back, I silently thanked my husky friend for the free upgrade.

Play games

Your house doesn't have to be big for a successful and noisy game of Hide and Seek to be lots of fun. Chutes and Ladders, slapjack, or doing puzzles together will give you hours of fun with your girl. Avoid the temptation to always watch television together. That does little to enhance your ability to interact.

Not every game you play with your girl needs to be store-bought, either. For example, you can play the toes-and-fingers game. The first time we played it, we were on a family vacation. For some reason, we started comparing the relative length of our fingers. Each person held up his or her hand with the fingers standing right next to each other, taking-an-oath style. We discovered that my index finger is shorter than my ring finger, and my middle finger is the longest, but that the pattern was different with each of us. Then we decided to check out our toes, so we took off our socks, laid on our backs next to each other, and held our feet aloft.

> *Avoid the temptation to always watch television together. That does little to enhance your ability to interact.*

Guess what—our toes were different, too. I was the only one with a second toe longer than my big toe. Missy's little toe looked like a sprout on a potato you've left in the basement too long. I can still see us lying there comparing our toes, and it still makes me laugh.

On car trips, we made up all kinds of fun games. We would divide the car into two teams, the left side and the right side. Then we'd silently count cows, sheep, and horses. Cows were one point, sheep were five points, and horses were 10. Dogs, cats, and birds didn't count. You could count only the animals on your side. However, if you spotted a graveyard on your opponents' side, all their animals were "dead," and they would have to start over.

The alphabet game was also a favorite. Starting with "Ready, go," each person in the car would silently collect each of the letters of the alphabet from road signs. They had to be gathered in order—you'll find yourself praying for "j's" and "q's"—and no fair turning around to see signs on the other side of the road. That would have made it unfair for the driver. We made this rule because I'm such a competitor that I might have wrecked the car looking for a missing letter . . . like "p" for paramedic! The first person to "z" would holler out the letter, and the game was over.

Sometimes on trips, we would "collect" license plates from as many states as possible.

Laugh at yourself

Both our girls were school cheerleaders. Occasionally they would coerce me into learning one of their favorite cheers. Knowing my level of coordination was no match for that of limber and graceful girls, I would still give it a try. Those sessions always ended with hilarious laughter directed at this clumsy, inflexible dad trying to put all the moves of the cheer together. Tough as some of those ego-busting adventures were, I tried to make sure I laughed, too.

The girls always loved it when I told stories of my childhood. Sometimes on trips I would tell them some of the silly things I did as a little boy or teenager. For some reason, they loved to hear about the times I got in trouble. They'd laugh at my foolishness, and, because a lot of years have passed since I did the stupid thing I was telling them about, I'd laugh, too.

Several years ago, it dawned on me that life was getting too serious. I was deeply entrenched in the perils of keeping a small business afloat. All my working life, payroll day had been a happy day. But since I was now one of the owners, payroll was a treacherous day. The one day every two weeks when I should have had a happy face, I looked worse than usual. My family started to remind me that I was "looking too serious these days."

So, the next time I was in our local bookstore, I wandered over to the humor section. Rifling through the selection of books, I discovered some pretty funny stuff. I bought several titles. In reading those books and the many others I've bought since, I discovered that although I *wanted* to be fun (and funny), I just didn't have enough material. Those books were just what I needed.

I also bought *The Far Side* daily calendar and a few books of Gary Larson's collections. Describing one of his bizarre cartoons to my family can be as funny as reading it for the first time.

Reading such material brought something important to my conscious mind: There are lots of funny things about *me,* and the same will be true of you. I had never thought about that before. But visiting those humorists and seeing them laugh at themselves and at life as it really is gave me permission to uncover those things about myself that are, well, laughable.

Like forgetting things.

Ralph and Mildred were, as they say, in their sunset years. After their children were grown, they moved from Minnesota to Florida (of course) in order to thaw out.

Early one afternoon, Mildred called Ralph in from the patio. "Ralph," she started, "would you go down to the grocery store for me?"

"Sure, Mildred, what do you need?"

"Milk and eggs," came her reply.

Turning on his heel, Ralph headed for the carport.

"Ralph," Mildred warned, "I think you ought to write it down."

Ralph was insulted. "Mildred, milk and eggs? How tough can it be? Of course I don't need to write it down."

"Okay, Ralph, but I think you ought to write it down." Then, as an afterthought, Mildred added, "Oh, and I also need a pound of bacon."

Driving to the local Safeway, Ralph rehearsed the grocery list: "Milk, eggs, and bacon. Eggs, bacon, and milk. Bacon, eggs, and milk." Ralph was so confident that he was juggling the words without dropping a single one.

After parking his car in the vast parking lot, he walked to the store and stepped on the "Welcome to Safeway" rubber mat. The door swung open.

Nobody knows exactly why—maybe it was the automatic door-opening mechanism—but the moment he stepped onto the shiny, green-and-white-checked vinyl tiles of the grocery store, his mind went completely blank. Panic swept over him. *What was it I was supposed to get for Mildred?* he thought. But try as he might, it just wouldn't come back. He rifled through his memory like a desperate kid looking for a special treasure at the bottom of his toy box. Nothing.

For the next 30 minutes, Ralph wandered the aisles, looking for something—anything—that would jog his memory. No luck.

Since his fruitless journey terminated in the freezer section, Ralph thought he'd at least buy a half gallon of vanilla ice cream. *I'll keep this trip from being a total waste,* he resolved.

Walking into the kitchen from the carport, Ralph dropped the paper sack on the counter with a thunk. Mildred, detecting that something might be wrong, walked to the bag. Without even looking at Ralph, she opened it. Slowly pulling out the ice cream, she asked her forlorn and embarrassed husband, "Ralph . . . Ralph, how could you? You forgot the chocolate syrup."

Like Ralph and Mildred, I'm getting old. I'm "losing" things in my mind. Half sentences followed by long pauses, followed by "I forgot what I was going to say," are now as common as carpet. The hair on my skinny legs is falling off and reappearing in my nose and ears. My eyesight is failing. Without my reading glasses, most books look like lined paper. I get *really* tired at 8:30 in the evening. And I enjoy watching golf on TV. This week it's "The Buick-Frito-Lay-Tidy-Bowl Classic," and the first prize is $160 million.

What are my choices in reaction to the fact that I'm getting older? I can get sour. I can get angry that my body can't do what it used to be able to do. Or I can laugh at myself. I can find humor in the fact that I actually enjoy coupon shopping at the grocery store and that a "full evening" sometimes means watching "Headline News" three times in a row.

In his wonderful and refreshing book *Laugh Again,* Charles Swindoll says it like this: "Far too many adults I know are serious as a heart attack. They live with their fists tightened, and they die with deep frowns. They cannot remember when they last took a chance or risked trying something new. The last time they tried something really wild, they were nine years old. I ask you, where's the fun? Let's face it, you and I are getting older—it's high time we stop acting like it!"

And as our daughters grow older themselves, my ability to enjoy growing older, to laugh at myself, gives them less fear about the same thing—getting older. Perhaps it even gives them the chance to find humor in their own shortcomings, foibles, and idiosyncrasies today.

Laugh with your daughter.

BUILDER'S CHECKLIST

1. *Retell the stories that last a lifetime:* There are situations we've gotten ourselves into that make great "material" for the rest of our lives. Don't forget to reminisce with your family about those fateful situations. It's great fun.

2. *Ask yourself if you are fun to live with:* Several years ago, a friend said to me, "Every once in a while, I stop and think what it must be like to live with me." What a good thing to do!

3. *Remember the three rules for laughter:*
   a. Laugh *with* your girl, never *at* her. Play "grizzly bear," buy riddle books, and rent silly videos.
   b. Laugh at circumstances. Tell tales of your own growing up, or go camping!
   c. Laugh at yourself. Let your mistakes and foibles be the stuff of family humor. It'll be okay. You'll survive!

4. *Have fun with your daughter:* Turn off the television. Get out a game and play it with your girl. There are plenty to choose from, regardless of her age . . . or yours.

CHAPTER EIGHT

Faith:

Jesus loves me,
this I know

"The great door sighs, then opens, and a child enters the church

and kneels at the front pew. The Maker of the Universe has smiled.

He made the church for this one interview."

DANIEL SARGENT

Given a choice, I'd rather not attend neighborhood parties—and I don't mean getting together with friends who live within shouting distance of our front yard. Those are fun. What I'm referring to are the all-neighborhood-from-sea-to-shining-sea-Honey-do-I-have-to-go parties. First, I'm essentially a shy person. Over the years, I've learned not to be shy in most situations. But given a choice, I'd rather spend the evening with Bobbie, a few close friends, or just plain alone.

Second, the conversation at those parties is always the same. Question one: "Now, which house do you live in?" Answer: "The Cape Cod at the end of Winding Way." Question two: "And what do you do?" Answer: The shortest description possible of what I do.

After I've answered those questions as many times as I can possibly handle, I look for my wife and beg her to go home with me or even to let me go home alone.

Occasionally at one of those gatherings, someone finds out that I teach a Sunday school class. He'll ask which church we attend, and then he'll make a valiant attempt to identify with this "religious" person he's just encountered.

"You know, my cousin married a guy whose next door neighbor has a sister-in-law, and I think she's one of those." Then he adds, "I've heard she's such a nice person." Yeah, but she probably slaughters innocent chickens with her bare hands during full moons.

Once your poor neighbor has made this point of "religious" contact, he's off to get another drink and find someone normal.

Okay, what I've just told you is a slight exaggeration. But it *is* the way I used to feel about parties where I didn't know most of the guests. And, I'm afraid, it's the way lots of "nonreligious" people feel about bumping into Christians at parties.

I remember when Billy Graham used to make appearances on "The Tonight Show." He was always the first guest. Johnny Carson would be respectful and kind. Dr. Graham would also be respectful and kind. Then, as soon as the conversation was over, Johnny would say regretfully, "Unfortunately, Dr. Graham cannot be with us for the whole show . . . but, it was *certainly* a pleasure having you with us tonight!"

Pleasant and sincere handshakes were exchanged, and Dr. Graham was gone. Then the real fun started.

The Astro-Boring-Dome

Twenty years ago, my family visited the Astrodome. Walking into a building that size was unbelievable—*indoor* baseball. I remember gazing at the superstructure in absolute amazement. I also remember asking the guide if pop flies wouldn't just bounce off that ceiling.

She assured me they rarely do.

As part of the tour, they led our group into a small theater for a multimedia slide show. We were treated to a look at how the Astrodome was built—my favorite part—and how many different kinds of activities it could hold. We saw great action shots of rodeos, baseball games, tractor pulls (we were in Texas, remember), football games, and rock concerts. The music behind these slides was exciting and loud. We got the idea that this building certainly did hold a lot of thrilling and fun events.

Then the music faded into what sounded like an old hymn, played by the lovely minister's wife on a cheap, manual pump organ in some clapboard country church. Over this nice, unobtrusive, and flat music, the announcer told us that the Astrodome is so versatile that it's even used for religious services.

I remember feeling sick. *Why,* I thought, *isn't faith seen as just a normal part of life? Why do they have to drop the fun out of the music and portray Christians as, well, a little different? Compared to the rest of life, basically boring?*

Driving away from the Astrodome that day, Bobbie and I made a simple resolve: We will make our faith an everyday, normal thing. Our daughters will see us treat our love for God as part of our daily routine—not some clumsy diversion from real life.

So that's what we did.

A Daughter Who Loves God

Here's the bottom line: Your task is to build a little girl into a well-balanced woman who loves God. And how do you get there? Here are some ideas.

Thank God for her conception

> *Your task is to build a little girl into a well-balanced woman who loves God.*

Pregnancy is, more often than not, something to be avoided. We spend billions of dollars finding more and more reliable ways to keep from having children. In chapter 1, I told our story of conceiving far earlier in our marriage than we ever would have planned. I mentioned our friends' predictably shocked responses. Frankly, they were out of order.

Not only is conception something to be celebrated, but of all God's miracles, this one has been referred to for thousands of years as a specific sign of His "blessing"!

If you adopted your daughter, her conception is no less spectacular than if you and your wife had conceived her yourselves. In fact, in your case, God made *two* important choices: "To whom should I send this new life, and to whom should I give the privilege of nurture and growth?" Congratulations on being chosen as this girl's general contractor!

King David wrote one of the most important descriptions of this miracle in Psalm 139. He used the metaphor of "knitting together" to illustrate the way God forms and blends the delicate fibers of a developing baby. It's an incredible thing.

Thank God for sending this girl your way. Celebrate the miracle of conception.

Publicly promise to build your daughter

Some churches offer baby dedication. Some christen or baptize infants. But it's essentially the same thing: As her dad, you are publicly acknowledging that this little girl is a gift—on loan—from God. And you promise to bring her up in the faith.

You must do this in front of lots of people you know—people who, hopefully, love you enough to remind you of this promise; friends who would, at some later time, dare to challenge your activity when it seems to be drifting from this pledge.

The Book of Order that guides our particular denomination puts it this way: "The baptism of children witnesses to the truth that God's love claims people before they are able to respond in faith themselves. Those presenting children for baptism shall provide nurture and guidance within the community of faith and assume the responsibility of active church membership." Well said.

In fact, when a baby is brought before our church, the minister asks the members to signify that they promise to "assist the parents in the child's Christian nurture" by raising their right hand. It's an acknowledgment that building your daughter's faith will be a cooperative effort.

When you bring your little girl to the front of your church, promising to be an example of a godly man and asking your friends to be examples as well, you're putting the world on notice: I'm going to be a Christian father, I need some help from you, and I expect us to hold each other accountable on this one.

Present her to God publicly.

Teach your daughter to pray

If conversation between you and your daughter (chapter 4) is critical to effectively building your relationship with each other, teaching your daughter to talk to God will be just as critical to her building a meaningful relationship with Him.

Should you feel inadequate about exactly how to do this, ask a clerk at your local Christian bookstore. There are many wonderful books that will be of help to you. But regardless of how you go about it, teach your daughter to pray. Show her how to do this out loud. Teach her by doing it with her.

Several years ago, our older daughter was teaching fifth grade at a Christian school in Charlotte. Classes would begin each day with a prayer time. Missy asked each student for requests, and then she would invite anyone to be a part of the prayer time—to pray out loud.

One morning, a boy began praying for his dog. He asked God to keep his dog, Rascal, from getting run over by cars on the busy street where he and his family lived. Then he asked the Lord to help Rascal get rid of his ringworm. This is only humorous, of course, if you're neither Rascal nor the ringworm.

What fun to hear that a child is so comfortable with God that he can bring his most important concerns boldly to God's attention!

Here are a few guidelines to help you with teaching your girl to pray:

Praise and thank you's. When you pray with your girl, help her to always begin by thanking God for His goodness. If she's young when you start this, you're going to hear God get thanked for a whole lot of interesting things: birds, flowers, Grandma, a new box of Cap'n Crunch cereal. And that's okay. Let her roll. The older she gets, the more meaningful these "thank you's" will become. You're helping her to see that everything she has—including life itself—is a precious gift from God's hand.

Please forgive me's. You probably won't have too much difficulty with this, since most little girls have a great deal of sensitivity about their own shortcomings. But it's still important that you help her identify specific "forgive me's." "Forgive me for not sharing my toys with Jennifer" when she's three will translate to seeking God's forgiveness when life gets a lot more complex and dangerous.

Warning: Teaching your daughter to confess her sin is not about beating her up with how awfully she has acted. Please hear me on this. This is simply a way for her to begin, at an early age, to "notice" those things in her life that are out of order and to understand her need for the comforting forgiveness of a loving heavenly Father.

And remember, she will be learning this from you. In other words, she will hear you seeking God's forgiveness for your sin when you pray together.

Requests. Like her list of "thank you's," this might be a long one: "Bless Uncle Fred and Aunt Blanche, bless my dolls and teddy bears, bless my mommy and my daddy [Amen], bless my older sister in school, help Stephanie to get over the flu, please give us a sunny day tomorrow for the picnic . . ." Again, it's okay. Let this roll.

Your daughter is learning that God is a God of blessing—of good and perfect gifts.

And, finally . . . It's a good idea to help her close the prayer with one more statement of "thank you."

There you have it. Don't be embarrassed to actually *teach* this. If it means having her repeat phrases after you, that's okay. If it means helping her to do it right immediately after she's finished with a prayer, that's okay, too. In no time, she'll get the hang of it.

You've taught your daughter the importance of talking to God, and you've given her some helpful instruction on how to do it. This is very good.

Hint: If you're looking for times to pray, there are two "for sures." One is at mealtimes. Of course, you may not do more than thank God for the food, but make this a habit. Three times a day, you're reminding your daughter of God's tangible goodness and blessing. The second "for sure" is bedtime. This will be the best place for you to take a little more time and walk through the four steps listed above.

Teach your daughter to pray.

Teach your daughter to sing

When it comes to teaching your child to sing, the clerk at your Christian bookstore will be a big help once again. You'll find a huge selection of tapes and CDs that will teach your daughter songs lifting up the values that are important to you. Two or three times through these songs and she'll have them memorized. You'll hear her singing them to herself. As the words sink into her heart, they will be like reinforcing steel in the concrete of her character.

In addition to the songs you buy, you can also teach her little songs on your own. Of course, there are the old standbys, "Jesus Loves Me" and "Jesus Loves the Little Children."

There are also simple songs like:

God is so good, God is so good, God is so good, He's so good to me.

Then there are verses you can add:

> "He gave us Grandma, He gave us Grandma,
> He gave us Grandma, He's so good to me."

The possibilities are endless:

> "He gave us _____ (your daughter's name) . . ."
> "He gave us Mommy . . ."
> "He gave us Daddy (my personal favorite) . . ."

You might want to have your daughter learn some of the great, old hymns of the church, too. "Great Is Thy Faithfulness," "Praise to the Lord, the Almighty," and "A Mighty Fortress Is Our God," for example, are filled with incredible truths.

Music is going to be an important part of your daughter's life. It's the language of her generation, symbolizing the thinking of a culture. When she's old enough to get a stereo for her own room, you're going to be concerned about her tastes in that musical "language." This is an almost universal situation. Dads are a little—or a lot— worried about their daughter's selection of music. So when she's young, give her some of the really good stuff. It will help her as she makes musical judgments later.

Teach her to sing.

Teach your daughter to give

Spiritually speaking, there may not be a more important habit for your daughter to acquire than giving her money to the church. Again, this is something she's going to need to learn from you, so here's an idea: Let your daughter see you put something in the offering plate every time it passes.

Further, give her something to put into the offering when she's small. When she begins to earn her own money, be matter-of-fact about it, but remind her to give. There are many wonderful causes, such as caring for the poor or inner-city ministries, that your daughter could give to, even if it's just a few pennies a week. (Why not sponsor a "little sister" for your girl from another part of the world? One of our favorite organizations for this kind of thing is Compassion International. Their phone number is 1-800-336-7676. For $24 a month, you can connect your daughter to another little girl, providing her with love and care that will change her life. You'll also receive a picture of the child. Put it in a frame next to your daughter's bed, and remind her that God's love reaches everywhere.)

The Bible doesn't say there's anything wrong with money. What it clearly says is that it is foolish to *love* money. In fact, it warns that if we start loving our money, evil will have a superb chance to take root. Showing your daughter how to give generously will demonstrate that you know how to not love your money.

Buy her a Bible of her own

Many churches give children a Bible when they enter the third grade. There are often ceremonies in "big church" where the kids come forward to receive their Bibles. In most cases, these are grown-up Bibles, page after page of difficult-to-read, tiny, black words on white paper.

If that is literally her first Bible, you've missed a fantastic opportunity. Although it may be only a symbol before she's old enough to read, having a Bible of her own will help her understand that, at any age, this faith can actually be hers. Again, a quick visit to a Christian bookstore will help you find just the right Bible for her.

Give her the pride of having her own Bible. And have her name imprinted on the outside if you can. It's *hers*. And when you read to your daughter, read out of *her* Bible. Let her understand that the Book she's carrying around is filled with wonderful truth—truth that can be her very own.

Teach your daughter Bible verses

I've waited until now to tell you about my mother. She's an angel. This is not an exaggeration.

One week during the summer of 1976, Bobbie and I asked if my parents would take care of Julie while we vacationed in Missouri with friends. They said that they'd be glad to.

We returned to my parents' house late on a Saturday afternoon, and after all the we-missed-you's and thanks-for-taking-care-of-Julie's were finished, my mother said, "Robert and Bobbie, Julie has something to tell you."

With a huge smile on her face, Julie turned toward us and began to recite:

A - "All we like sheep have gone astray."
B - "Be ye kind one to another."
C - "Children obey your parents, for this is the right thing to do."
D - "Don't fret or worry, it only leads to harm."
E - "Every good and perfect gift is from above . . ."

Standing there in front of us, Julie recited 26 Bible verses, all the way from "All we like sheep" to "Zacchaeus, you come down." We were stunned. We were also deeply grateful that my mother had planted those verses in our daughter's heart. Three months later, Julie turned two!

As we drove back to our house, Bobbie and I decided to keep it up. So we—Bobbie mostly—helped the girls memorize lots and lots of Bible verses. In fact, she got so serious about it that she made a rule: No Bible, no breakfast.

Please believe me, this was all in fun. There were no morning furrowed brows or angry directives on this—"You memorize Ecclesiastes or you starve." We made a game of it—like checkers or Scrabble.

I suppose we'll never know how important those verses have been in our girls' lives, but I do know King David promised that "hiding" God's Word in a person's heart helps him—or her—defend against sin (see Ps. 119:11). That's a good reason all by itself, don't you think?

> *Talk about God as though knowing Him is a simple fact, not something mysterious or puzzling.*

Pour the Scriptures into your daughter.

Talk about God

On those never-go-on-errands-alone weekend trips to The Home Depot, when you're talking and patting your girl's knee, include God. For example, as you're driving along and you see a pretty tree, say, "Oh, Honey, look at the beautiful tree. Isn't God wonderful to have created something like that for us to enjoy?"

She'll say, "Yes, Daddy." And that'll be all.

Do not add anything to it. Please don't say, "You know, it's like Reverend Smith said on Sunday morning—at the 8:30 worship service and again at 11:00 . . ."

That's not normal.

Just say something about God, then follow it with something ordinary like, "Why don't you go ahead and tie your shoe so you don't trip over the laces when we get to the store." Talk about God as though knowing Him is a simple fact, not something mysterious or puzzling.

Give your daughter an extended Christian family

If your girl is young, begin praying that God will send her other Christian adults who will love her for "free." These are people who love God, like you, but they're not teachers ("Did you finish your homework?"), coaches ("Take another lap"), extended family ("When your dad was little, he used to . . ."), or surrogate parents ("Clean your room").

These "free" adults will do almost as much to shape your daughter's life and thinking as you. There are lots of good places to find folks like this, but your church is the best. You can also locate these adults in Young Life, Youth for Christ, Fellowship of Christian Athletes, and countless Christian summer camping programs. If you're really lucky, you'll find one in your neighborhood.

What you pray for is that these people will occasionally say to your daughter, "You know, your dad is right." That can be a powerful thing.

When we lived in Texas, Bobbie met Charlotte Mitchell at a Bible study. Although they didn't know each other well, Bobbie called Charlotte and asked if she and her husband would be able to take care of four-year-old Julie while we were out of town for a week-long trade show. Charlotte agreed.

As it turned out, Charlotte and David Mitchell were gifts to us. The Christian attitudes and values they underscored in Julie's heart were priceless. Even today, the memory of her week with the Mitchells fills Julie with a reminder of what God can do in other families.

Give your daughter a Christian family beyond your own. You won't be sorry.

Give your daughter an opportunity to teach

If you visit a church nursery or preschool Sunday school class, you'll notice something. In addition to the regular, adult teachers, there are also "helpers." More often than not, these "extras" are charged with duties like picking up toys or taking the little ones to the potty.

Encourage your daughter, as soon as she's old enough, to volunteer for that kind of duty. As she works with the younger children, she'll find herself on the receiving end of honest inquiries about life. And relationships. And God. As your daughter works through answers for those inquisitive little minds, she'll be sealing her own ideas and thinking about such things.

Being a "teacher" will also give her good questions to bring to you. As soon as she stumps you with a tough one (you won't have to wait long for this), you can search for an answer together.

Give your girl an opportunity to teach.

Bless your daughter

Depending on your spiritual training and background, this one may take some getting used to, but please hear me out. The Old Testament is full of stories about fathers giving a blessing to their children. In fact, one of the best-selling Christian books in the 1980s was *The Blessing*, written by Gary Smalley and Dr. John Trent. In a nutshell, the concept is that parents have a responsibility to provide verbal "blessings" to their children.

Centuries ago, people would not have had to be reminded of this concept. It was a common thing. In fact, people spoke blessings to each other when they met on the sidewalk. "Peace to you" was a lot more common than "Hey, what's up?"

Giving and receiving "blessings" is just a good idea.

I have no idea how this got started in our family, but for many years, after we say good-bye to our daughters, we've added, "The Lord be with you." They return the statement with "The Lord be with you, too."

In a moment of verbal interchange, we've given each other a

blessing. It's a comforting and inspiring way to say good-bye.

Verbally bless your daughter.

Give your daughter an "awe" for God

Think about this: When you and your daughter are talking to or about God, you are literally referring to the eternal Creator of the universe. This person is not only more important than Tom Cruise, Amy Grant, or Orel Hershiser, but He *made* those people, using dust as His raw material.

Remind her of God's majesty by an occasional mention of His creative genius. Let your daughter know that when you pray, sometimes you kneel down because you're so honored to be in God's presence. Every once in a while, let her join you on your knees. She'll get the picture.

In February 1987, Bobbie and I had a chance to visit Vice President George Bush at his official Washington residence. We were told this was going to be an intimate gathering of fewer than 50 people, and we were excited to meet the man who was, as they say, one heartbeat away from the most powerful job in the world.

That morning, as we were getting dressed in our hotel room, I practiced what I was going to say to Mr. Bush as I shook his hand. "Good afternoon, Mr. Vice President," I rehearsed in my deepest radio-announcer voice, firmly shaking his hand. "It's an honor to meet you." Over and over I repeated my lines. By the time we were standing in line to meet this very important person, I was ready.

When we got to Mr. Bush, an aide officially introduced us: "Mr. Vice President, this is Mr. and Mrs. Robert Wolgemuth from Nashville, Tennessee."

I nervously stuck out my hand, and, with a voice that sounded exactly like a prepubescent boy's, I chirped, "Hi there, I'm Robert."

We both laughed, and I tried again, this time sounding a little more like myself.

Day after day, I speak to God. I helped my daughters speak to Him as well. It's an overwhelming thing—being in the presence of this kind of greatness.

The most important thing we can do to help develop a daughter's personal faith is to give her a glimpse of what it is to actually *be* in God's presence. Once that's firmly planted in her heart, most everything else will take care of itself—including her conduct, which we'll talk about in the next chapter.

Building a House for God

In October 1982, on an unusually balmy evening, Bobbie and I were on our way to a weekly Bible study with a few other couples from our church. As we got closer to our friends' house, we noticed a yellow glow in the sky not too far from where we were. Hopelessly curious person that I am, I took a little detour.

Over the years, I had seen buildings on fire. Mostly I had seen smoke coming from upstairs windows, with a few flames here and there. But this night, I saw a house on *fire.* The flames were shooting 50 feet into the air. The crackling and popping sounded like something from camp, only on a much grander scale. Sparks completely filled the night sky.

Standing on the curb across from the inferno, I remember thinking, *Whoever lives in this house won't sleep tonight. How could they? In a few minutes, their beloved home will be completely gone.*

Regardless of who built your house, it has something in common with mine. They've been built, for the most part, with flammable materials. The careless use of matches or a stove that blows up will turn our homes into towering mountains of flame.

In the Psalms, King David made an important observation about your family's "contractor": "Unless the LORD builds the house, its builders labor in vain" (Ps. 127:1).

Building your daughter—and your home—with a solid faith is about using "materials" that are completely "fire-retardant." The eternal values that come with directing your daughter toward a God who loves her will help you build a home that lasts.

BUILDER'S CHECKLIST

1. *Make your faith "normal":* One of the most important things you can do is to make your faith a part of your daily routine.

2. *Teach your daughter to pray:* Go ahead and teach her, just as you taught her to tie her shoes. A prayer should include:
   a. Praise and "thank you's"
   b. "Please forgive me's"
   c. Requests
   d. One last "thank you"

3. *Review the ways to build godly character in your daughter:*
   a. Thank God for the miracle of your daughter's birth.
   b. Publicly promise to nurture her.
   c. Teach your daughter to pray.
   d. Teach your daughter to sing.
   e. Teach your daughter to give.
   f. Buy her a Bible of her own.
   g. Teach your daughter Bible verses.
   h. Talk about God.
   i. Give your daughter an extended Christian family.
   j. Give your daughter an opportunity to teach.

k. Bless your daughter.

l. Give her an "awe" for God.

4. *Let her teach you:* Helping to build a solid faith in your daughter will have a profound influence on your own faith. Among other effects, as she gets older, you'll discover why Jesus commended the little children for the depth of their faith, because she'll teach you!

CHAPTER NINE

Conduct:
You be
the judge

"When you go out into the world, watch out for traffic,

hold hands, and stick together."

ROBERT FULGHUM

Let's say that you call me tomorrow morning to tell me you're going to be in my town next weekend. You ask if I might be free on Saturday afternoon to go for a drive, taking you on a little tour of Williamson County. I say it would be fine for you to come by. We set a time, I give you directions to my house, we say good-bye, and we hang up.

The following Saturday, at the appointed time, you pull into my driveway, and, since you're not still in high school, you actually get out of your car and meet me at the front door. We exchange greetings, I get a jacket, and we walk back down the sidewalk toward your car.

When we get to your car, I mention that I'd prefer riding in the backseat. Thinking it's a strange suggestion, you try to talk me out of it. But since this is my story and I'm making the rules, I prevail.

As we back out of the driveway, you feel silly—like a cab driver in your own car. You've never gone out with a friend who was sitting in the backseat. *This really feels weird,* you think.

Leaving my subdivision, I ask if you've ever driven around my town before. You say you haven't. I tell you I'll be happy to show you around. *But why is he sitting in the backseat?* you continue to wonder. You take a deep breath and do your best to get this unusual setup out of your mind.

When we come to the stop sign leading out of our subdivision, you pause. "Which way should I turn?" you ask.

"Oh, you just go ahead," I reply.

"But I don't know where I'm going," you counter.

"That's okay," I say. "I'll let you know."

You take a moment, look left and right, and turn left. I don't say anything.

In a mile or so, we come to a traffic light. It's red. While we're sitting there, waiting for the green, you ask, "Which way now?"

"You go ahead," I say. "I'll let you know."

The light turns green. Again you look left and right. Since most of the cars you're following turn left, you turn left, too. *Left worked last time,* you reason, *so maybe it'll work again.*

But the moment the car clears the intersection after your left turn, I lean forward and slap the right side of your face with my open hand. Hard. The impact of the blow sends your sunglasses flying.

You're so shocked that it takes a minute for you to say anything. But you gather your composure and glance over your shoulder. "What was that!" you exclaim.

"Wrong turn," I shoot back.

More than a little bewildered, you look for an opportunity to make a safe U-turn and head down the road in the correct direction.

For the next several hours, we tour my county. I never tell you where we're going or which way to turn at intersections. I only let you know, with my open hand, if you've made the wrong choice.

By the end of the afternoon, you have resolved that (a) this is the last time you're ever taking me on a drive, and (b) I'm a complete and worthless jerk. Good thinking on both accounts.

Welcome to the World of Being a Kid

Admittedly, the scenario I've just walked you through is ridiculous. Who would ever do such a thoughtless and contemptuous thing?

How could I have expected you to do any better unless I had told you, in advance, where we were going and the best way to get there?

You're way ahead of me, aren't you? What I'm describing is the way many children feel as they grow up with parents who seem to know where their kids are supposed to go, but the only real directions they give are those painful physical or verbal "slaps" when the children make wrong choices. And although you and I would never be as brutal and unfair as I was in our story, I assure you that what I've described is not an uncommon way to explain what it sometimes *feels* like to be a kid.

The Order Is Intentional

This chapter is about conduct—how your girl should act in certain situations. And it's purposely at the end of these last seven chapters about how to build a daughter.

Why? Because too often we want to focus on specific issues of conduct right away. We buy

> *Even if we've got a high-spirited, strong-willed girl, setting rules for conduct should be our last concern.*

books because we want answers. *Hey, I paid good money for this book. Don't waste my time with philosophical drivel—just tell me what to do and what not to do.*

But even if we've got a high-spirited, strong-willed girl, setting rules for conduct should be our *last* concern. If we try to make it first on our list, we'll spend most of our time "slapping" from the backseat.

Let's review the last several chapters, but in doing so, let's focus on how they relate, ultimately, to conduct.

Protection
Your role as the guiding and protecting "point person" in your girl's life is a given. You can't delegate it to anyone else. Even though

this parenting thing is a partnership with your wife, your job as the protecting dad is irreplaceable. You must know when to "parent" and when to "de-parent"—when to step in to protect and when to let her "learn a lesson." Without an understanding of your role in protecting, you may not have understood why you must be the one to administer the guidelines of conduct.

Conversation

In every situation you encounter with your daughter, your ability to openly "talk about it" will be the greatest guiding "device" you could employ. Good conversation releases the internal, secret pressure that builds toward foolish or dangerous conduct. If your daughter feels free to talk to you about what's really going on in her life, she'll stay out of serious trouble most of the time.

Affection

Your girl must feel the enveloping security of your physical and emotional "arms." She must know your tender touch and your affirming words. And these must come from you at times when there's no direct connection between her conduct and your loving support. You are affirming her *person,* not her *performance.*

Correction

Yes, this *is* about conduct. But it's about your conduct—personal discipline—in stark contrast to, or in support of, your attempts to be the disciplinarian. It's about toughness, consistency, and fairness. It's about your willingness to be "the bad guy" in order to build the gyroscope of discipline inside your daughter.

Laughter

More than anything else, fun-loving laughter helps you to be real. It's the cornerstone in the developing friendship between you and your daughter. Laughter gives you something to look forward to—it's a holiday you and your girl take from the serious rigors of making rules and setting guidelines. Laughter gives balance to a tough-to-face world.

Faith
Your job is to usher your girl into the presence of an awesome God, helping her to understand that the more she knows about Him—His justice and grace—the less emphasis there will need to be on the conduct "list." You will also need to let her see how your understanding of the same principle guides your behavior.

Begin with the End in Mind

In the first chapter, you read about Cousin Larry's Construction Company and the artist's rendering of a finished building project. That illustrated the importance of always focusing on the finished product rather than the often-frustrating details of the day to day.

Talking about conduct is almost always unpleasant, even dangerous. Without any context, it can sound as if you're placing conditions on your love: "I will love you more when your conduct is acceptable." However, as you build your daughter, your challenge is the same as Cousin Larry's Construction Company faced: Focusing not on the process (conduct) but on the payoff (completeness). Begin with the end in mind.

Speak to the goal you're attempting to reach
In chapter 5, I warned against complimenting other girls in areas where your daughter could never measure up—for example, in physical attributes like hair color and body shape. But the same principle can be applied from a positive point of view.

Compliment in areas where you *want* your daughter to excel—in places where she *can* achieve. For example, instead of talking about another girl's hair color or leg length, say to another child, "I couldn't help but notice how polite you were when you spoke to your mother." Say this in your daughter's presence.

Your goal is to build a polite and well-mannered daughter, and that's something she knows she can achieve. So you give her a glimpse of your priorities through your observation of another child.

Warning: Leave your comment just to the compliment. Don't turn to your girl and say anything about *her* conduct. Do *not* compare her manners to those of the girl you've just spoken to. If her conduct doesn't measure up at the moment, she'll get the message. No further analysis will be necessary from you.

Or you can look for opportunities to "catch" your daughter doing something right: "Thank you for helping Mrs. Jamison with baby Mary. She told me how much she appreciates your kindness."

You are painting a picture of what you have in mind for your own daughter, and you're "hanging" that picture in a place where she can see it. You're putting a high value on achievable goals, but you're letting her draw that conclusion herself.

This is a powerful thing.

Focus on negative consequences and positive rewards

You have four useful "allies" in illustrating the inescapable truths of cause and effect: your own experience, the experiences of your friends and acquaintances, the daily newspaper, and rewards.

Regarding your own experiences, there's no need to go into the sordid details. But you can usually talk openly about the unhappy *result* of past foolishness.

And again, there's no need to finish the story with, "So see, Honey, this is what will happen if you do such and such." Don't insult her by stating an obvious conclusion. Let her draw her own. It will make a much stronger impact on her if she has to think about it herself.

The experiences of your friends and acquaintances also provide a helpful backdrop for your reasons for good conduct.

Then, let your daughter see the daily newspaper. Because newspaper publishers are most interested in selling newspapers, they often put the most shocking or tragic stories on the front page. The message to your daughter will be clear: Activity always has results. Foolish conduct creates unhappiness and chaos. To avoid such consequences, avoid such conduct.

Your other ally is rewards. When your daughter is small, you'll be amazed at what she'll do for a page of stickers or a trip to her favorite frozen yogurt place. If her conduct warrants such a reward, she'll get it. If it doesn't, she won't.

Warning: Be certain that the rules are clear. "If you do thus and so, you'll get thus and so." Make the completion of the task and the achievement of the reward objective and completely up to her. When she's young, you may even want to post a list of her desired activities and potential rewards on the refrigerator. Also, be absolutely certain you have your wife's support on this, as well as on any other issues related to conduct. Don't present the plan to your daughter until there's unanimity among "the judges."

Help your daughter search for her own gifts

When I was growing up, the areas where a girl could excel were limited—basically, music and academics. So, not surprisingly, the valedictorians and singers were usually girls. Happily, we now live in a culture where the possibilities for your daughter's personal achievement are almost inexhaustible.

Your job is to help her find that special area where she can be a winner.

King Solomon said it this way, "Train up a child in the way he [she] should go . . ." In other words, your job is to mentor, or coach, your daughter according to her own particular bent, or skill set. The personal satisfaction of achievement, coupled with the accolades of her friends, will do more to shape her conduct than any "list" you could ever create, even if your list were the best ever conceived.

To do this, you'll need to expose your girl to many different options when she's young: music, dance, sports, art, collectibles, drama, and so on. You'll discover that what you loved or achieved as a youngster may not interest her at all. Do your best to affirm every possibility—unless, of course, she develops an interest in building explosives in your garage.

Once she lands on her own "specialty," she'll blossom.

Okay, Okay, But What About "the List"?

Being a great daddy is a lot like being a successful manager in business. Your relationship with your subordinates is sound. There's trust and mutual support. They know exactly what they're supposed to do. Finally, you're close enough to the work to see—I didn't say "meddle in"—how well they're doing day to day, just in case there's a need for some midcourse correction.

In reading through the following list of "do's and don'ts," remember the wisdom of one of my favorite motivational speakers, Zig Ziglar: To be an effective parent, you must let your children know what you *expect* from them, and then you must be close enough to the action to be able to regularly *inspect* their work. Your success will depend on your ability to communicate clearly what is right and your diligence in making sure your daughter is following up.

Now, because every dad needs some help with specific situations, here are a few suggestions. Those that I believe are "hills worth dying on" are marked with an asterisk(*).

Disobedience*

Depending on your daughter's nature, her "ability" to disobey may come at an early age. You'll know she understands obedience — and disobedience — when you've asked her to do o 1ot do something and she hesitates, then does the opposite of what you asked.

Our baby Missy was crawling across the living room floor toward the fireplace. I said, "No, Missy." She stopped and turned toward me as if to say, *Are you talking to me? No, you must be referring to some other crawling child about to do something dangerous.* Then she continued to crawl away.

I quickly ran to her, picked her up, sat her on my lap, got her attention, and took an extended sequence of light swats at her diapered, well-protected bottom. She immediately cried, knowing I was displeased with what she had done. At that very early age, my daughter understood that disobedience is unacceptable. No discussion necessary.

In chapter 6, I talked about "the first time." Obeying is what the first time is about. Please don't wait on this one. Make it swift and sure every time. It won't be long before you will rarely have to punish for disobedience. The message will have been transmitted and received loud and clear: Don't disobey.

Long after our daughters were grown and gone, I was sitting in a doctor's waiting and waiting and waiting room, wondering if perhaps his assistant had meant 2:30 *tomorrow* afternoon.

While I waited, I people-watched. There were folks with bandages on their arms or faces, people with colds sniffling away, and a few who didn't look sick at all. I made up possible reasons for why they were there. Right next to me was a little girl, probably two years old. Her daddy was on the other side of her, apparently having drawn the short straw on taking his daughter to the doctor.

To say this girl was fidgety would be a gross understatement. She never stopped moving. She'd sit on the seat, move to the arm of the chair on my side, then switch to the arm on her daddy's side. Then she'd get down off the chair and crawl under it, looking for something, anything, to do.

After every one of her movements, this curly-headed perpetual-motion machine would hear her father say, "No, Ashley." She'd move; he'd say no. She would stop for one second, move again, and he'd say no again.

Was this disobedience? Technically, yes. Was it punishable? If you're talking about punishing the little girl, absolutely not. Why? Because she was literally incapable of doing *nothing*. So, instead of her dad droning on "No, No, No," he should have said, "Here, Ashley, let's play a game."

One of our favorites at such moments was "B.B. Bumblebee, I see something you don't see." With no props, we could keep a two-year-old busy for . . . well . . . several minutes! You go first and say, "B.B. Bumblebee, I see something you don't see, and it's red." Then you give your daughter a chance to look around the room and guess what red thing you might be looking at. When she gets it right, it's her turn.

Crying

There are two kinds of crying when your daughter is still very young. One means, "I am legitimately hungry, wet, or injured." That kind of crying is acceptable. Do whatever is necessary to remove the problem: Feed her, change her, or soothe her injury.

Then there's the other kind of crying that means, "I'm ticked off, I'm not getting my way, and this is how I'm going to get a little attention around here." We ignored this kind of crying until it went away, or we punished if it didn't. That, in turn, created a reason to cry—spanking—so then it could be soothed.

As your daughter grows, keep the rules about crying the same: Crying is permissible for legitimate reasons—hurt feelings, physical injury, sorrow. But crying should not be an acceptable method of gaining leverage to get her way or send a message to her parents.

In most states, it's illegal to flash your car's headlights for any reason other than to signal some kind of legitimate distress. I had a friend in high school who once saw a speed trap on the other side of the road and decided to alert oncoming traffic. Unfortunately for him, there was a speed trap on his own side of the highway in another mile or so, and when the policeman saw him flashing his lights, he pulled him over.

"Who do you think you are, Paul Revere?" was all the highway patrolman said to my friend. Then he gave him a stiff ticket.

Crying, like flashing headlights, should only be for signaling distress. Don't let it be used any other way.

Whining

Assuming there are no medical reasons to cause whining and pouting, they're usually a result of simple boredom. They often follow mindlessly staring at the television for hours on end.

When your daughter comes to you, talking with that annoying—blackboard-scraping—whine, tell her first that, as my wife used to say, "I can't understand what you're saying when you talk like that. Talk to me in a big-girl voice."

Then, two actions usually bring about a solution: (1) Turn off the TV, and (2) help her find something to do. Get creative. Have her help you in the garden. If you're a cook, have her help you in the kitchen. Take her to the store with you. Help her start a leaf collection. Buy some water colors and paintbrushes.

Get her good books to read, or buy her a cassette player of her own and some positive, character-building audio tapes. Again, you'll find an ample assortment at your local Christian bookstore.

Once you've done this a few times and your girl knows how to find something to do, challenge her to do so without you, the family-camp activities director, the next time.

Lying*

Like disobedience, lying must be nipped in the bud. A person who grows up not fully appreciating the importance of truth-telling is a person bound to live a painful life. Let your daughter know that dishonesty is absolutely unacceptable.

As our girls were growing up, we had a policy about truthfulness that you and your wife may want to discuss before you make it a house rule. But if you do this, it will reward your daughter for telling the truth.

Here's the policy: There will be no punishment if you tell the truth.

Of course, there may be unavoidable *consequences* for what your daughter has done—like hurting the little girl next door (taking her to the neighbor to ask forgiveness) and cheating on a test at school (a failing grade). But if the truth is told, there will be no direct punishment—spanking or loss of privileges.

This accomplishes two important things. First, it insures that the lines of communication between you and your girl will always be wide open. She will be rewarded for being truthful. (Isn't lying usually committed because of the fear of punishment? Then telling the truth ought to be rewarded.)

> *A person who grows up not fully appreciating the importance of truth-telling is a person bound to live a painful life.*

Second, because of the relationship you've established with your daughter through conversation, affection, and so forth, she will want to avoid disappointing you through misconduct.

In the New Testament, the apostle Paul reminded the Christians in the city of Corinth that Christ's love for them ought to "constrain" them. Other translations of that word include "arrest" and "straighten out."

Your relationship with your daughter and your love for each other will naturally have an "arresting" and "straightening out" effect on her behavior. Don't be afraid that the no-punishment-for-the-truth rule will turn into reckless behavior. Your mutual love will provide plenty of control.

Manners*

Teaching your daughter good manners gives her a priceless gift that will last a lifetime. In chapter 4, we addressed the way to teach your daughter to greet adults: "Nice to meet you, Dr. Holland." And as I mentioned, the "payoff" that Dr. Holland and other grown-ups will give her will more than "compensate" her for her effort.

Table manners. We have friends who, like us, have two daughters. Every once in a while, maybe two or three times a year, they have a "formal" dinner at their own home—candles, the "good" china, classical music—the whole thing. They call it "Going to the White House." And although it's treated like a game, it's a serious way of teaching their young girls how, when the time is appropriate, to act properly. Manners are not taught in most schools. If your girl doesn't learn everything from how to pass a plate to how to set the table at your house, she won't learn it.

"Yes, Sir" and "Yes, Ma'am." I know there will be an honest difference of opinion on this issue (like maybe you think I'm living during the time of the Crusades), but when Bobbie and I moved to

the South, we noticed that some youngsters used "Sir" and "Ma'am" when addressing adults. We really liked the respect those terms communicated, so we asked that when the girls spoke to adults, including us, they would use "Sir" and "Ma'am." Because they were quite young, they had no trouble complying.

We made this decision because we felt that encouraging our girls to use those terms was an important symbol of respect. But using words that honored others also had an impact on our children's *self*-respect. Adults would invariably speak graciously to our daughters in response to being referred to as "Sir" or "Ma'am." Respect given was respect *received,* and respect *received* was respect *believed.*

In the classic movie *My Fair Lady,* Professor Henry Higgins changed Eliza Doolittle's life with a single thing: changing the way she spoke. Teaching your daughter how to speak graciously and courteously will have the same impact.

Telephone manners. Have you noticed that there are phones everywhere? As I recall, Ozzie and Harriet Nelson had only one, and it was in the kitchen. And since Harriet was always in the kitchen and her apron was always perfectly ironed, she usually answered the phone. Talking about telephone manners with Ricky and Dave Nelson would not have been all that important.

Now there are phones in nearly every room in your home. They're also in many people's cars and boats. So, since your daughter is going to answer the phone, teach her how to do it properly.

(Phone rings.) "Hello, this is Missy."

"Hello, Missy, may I speak to your dad?"

"Yes, just a minute please."

Missy sets the phone down and comes to get me. She does *not* holler at the top of her lungs, "DAAAAAAAD."

We didn't teach our girls to ask who was calling. A young girl is probably not going to be a good screener anyway, so don't subject your calling friends to this interrogation.

Public places manners. We broke "going out" into two categories: kid things and adult things. When we went out as a family or when it was a church social with lots of other families, that was a "kid thing." At those times, it was not only acceptable to act like a kid, but it was a requirement—have fun and enjoy yourself with the other children.

However, if the function was a "mostly adult" affair, like a wedding or church service, the order of the day was to "act like an adult." In fact, when we would arrive at such events, I would say to the girls, "Look around. What kind of people do you see?"

They would reply, "Grown-ups."

Then I would say, "Okay, then how are we going to act?"

And the predictable—and correct—response was, "Like adults."

What this primarily meant was that the girls stayed with their mother and me. The temptation was strong to run up and down the aisles after the service, or to buzz through the hazelnuts on the punch-and-cookies table, but because this was an "adult event," we didn't do those things. *Before* you arrive at these functions, be certain you have made your expectations clear.

Your level of resolve on these issues of manners will keep this area from becoming a battlefield. There's no need to be angry in verbalizing your expectations to your daughter. But she needs to realize that when you say "This is the way you're going to act," that's exactly what you mean.

On your way home from extra-serious and extra-long adult events, when your daughter has been very good, tell her she acted like a princess. Then stop for frozen yogurt and let her get sprinkles on hers!

Messiness

Although it's true that no kid ever died of a messy room, the thing about living in a family is that one person's thoughtlessness will often affect someone else. We have friends who referred to leaving a mess, even in their own bedroom, as "smoke." They encouraged their children not to do it, since everyone else had to "smell" the messy person's "smoke," and that wasn't fair to the others.

Another dad told me that he asked his children to stop in the doorway and turn around before they walked out of a room. If someone walking into the room would be able to tell they had been there, they were asked to go back and "remove all evidence."

Finishing homework

It has probably been a long time since you were in grade school. You may have forgotten how fidgety and impatient you became at the end of the school day, anxious to get out of there.

Here is where you can begin to help your daughter with time management. Give her some time for herself right after school. Don't make her jump right into her homework. But before dinner, have her get some of it finished. Then, in the evening, she's not facing all of it without having gotten a head start.

If you think your girl has too much homework, talk to her teacher. You may find that your daughter isn't getting her work done at school. But if you discover the teacher thinks she's still in her own Ph.D. program down at the university, respectfully encourage her to back off a little.

We have good friends who visited their son's teacher. After learning that the teacher treated lots of homework like some sort of sacred rite, my friend said, "You have possession of my son for seven hours every day. I promise that I'll monitor my son in the evening, insuring that he puts in one solid hour of homework a day. After that, he belongs to me."

Though that sounds reasonable and fair to me, try it at your own risk.

Selecting friends*

The impact of friends will be another "seesaw" in your daughter's life—little effect when she's small, growing to be fairly significant as she gets older.

First and foremost, you need to know who her friends are. As much as is possible, have her friends to *your* home. Doing this will give you a good idea of who these other children are and what kind of influence they might have on your girl.

Because of the way things are these days, having other children to your house may be the only chance they'll have to see what a Christian home looks like. Imagine the impact your family could have on some youngster! This is how my wife came to the faith—playing with a girl in the neighborhood, visiting her home, and discovering what it was to live in a Christian home. The impact of this Christian family eventually led my wife's entire family to church, then to personal faith in Christ.

Second, talk to your daughter about her choice of friends, especially if some of those choices are giving you concern. This must be handled carefully, not because you don't have the "right" or are in some way afraid to discuss these issues, but because you want your daughter, as she grows up, to begin making her own sound friendship decisions. If you're making them for her, you're not teaching her anything except "What Dad says, goes." That's not a helpful lesson for her to have learned, because when she's on her own, you won't be around to say anything. Then what will she do? That's right, make bad choices.

As you're discussing her friends with your daughter, do two important things:

Make "I" statements. Talk to your daughter about how *you* felt when you were around her friend. For example, "When you were playing with Ginger, it seemed to me that she was always taking things from the other children. Seeing a child who acts selfishly makes me very sad." Or, "When I talked to Cindy, I noticed she said sassy things about her mother. That made me feel bad."

You're giving your daughter a chance to make the same observations you've made without feeling defensive. You're not saying, "You certainly do pick selfish, thoughtless friends to play with, don't you?" If you approach this delicate situation awkwardly, you'll have a battle on your hands. And you'll have earned it.

Ask questions. Once you've made certain observations, ask your daughter if she noticed the same things and how they made *her* feel. Listen carefully to her answers. What you're looking for is your girl's honest appraisal of this friend. If she shares some of your concerns, you may end the conversation with, "Do you think it might be a good idea for you to spend more time with your other friends and less time with Ginger or Cindy?"

Start this process as early as you can. Giving your daughter permission to honestly and openly discuss her friends with you when they're at the hopscotch stage will be a valuable "bridge" you can use when she's much older and the stakes are considerably higher.

Choosing and wearing clothes

Avoiding the temptation to put an asterisk next to this, let me simply say that I believe that what your daughter wears is an important issue.

Most girls, even if they're dressed in a way that communicates a disregard for what they look like, are *intentionally* dressed that way! But believing the adage "You act as you are dressed" to be true, let me encourage you to do the following:

As much as you can, give her approved "choices." There will come an age—it may be as young as two or three years old—when your daughter will have strong opinions about what she wears. She'll resist you or your wife telling her exactly what to wear. So give her a choice. Lay out two, three, or four outfits, and tell her that she may "choose any of these."

That way, even though she feels as if she's being given a choice, you can't go wrong.

Avoid extremes. You don't want your daughter to get her identity from what she wears. Ultimately, you want her to be known by her character.

For a short time, Missy went to a private, all-girls school. Every student wore the same outfit, with absolutely no room for individual creativity. At first, I thought that would be a problem for our daughter, but in no time, she literally "forgot" about her clothing. It was *not* an issue. It also was a real frustration-saver every morning during the formerly traditional what-should-I-wear-today discussions (battles).

The goal is to encourage your daughter to wear "the uniform" of her school. That is, don't allow her to make her clothes either a source of embarrassment—because you've forced her into "out of it" clothes—or a source of identity—because you've allowed her to step out of line, either overdressing or underdressing. Normally, you're against the whole notion of conformity, but in this situation, let her be comfortable with her clothes. Let her be stylish but not extreme, "matching" what most of her classmates are wearing. Then she'll forget about it.

Modesty. Here's where your experience as a man is your greatest asset. You have the right, even an obligation, to tell your daughter that something she's wearing could "communicate" the wrong thing to a boy. Most postpubescent girls have no idea about this. They may wear something provocative that they would call "cute." You can tell them that, to a boy, it's not "cute." It's an absolute, jaw-dropping turn-on.

Although it's easy to notice only when your daughter is wearing something "questionable," please be quick to tell her how wonderful she looks when she's wearing something conservative. An honest compliment from a boy (you) will be highly motivating to her.

> *You have the right, even an obligation, to tell your daughter that something she's wearing could "communicate" the wrong thing to a boy.*

Just between you and me, I detest bikinis. I don't mean that I just hate them; I mean that I *hate* them. Most bikinis are smaller than underwear! Do your best to "fight" bikinis by telling your daughter how nice she looks in a one-piece. It's too bad you can't go shopping with her when she's looking for a bathing suit. If you could, you'd probably notice that she's a little self-conscious modeling the ones sewn from material no larger than a credit card. That's good. Let her feel self-conscious. It might encourage her to moderate her thinking a little.

This may turn into Gettysburg between you and your girl. Don't let it. Try to be as nonadversarial as possible. Offer *suggestions.* Good luck.

Selecting music

Can we skip this one? No? Okay, let's talk about it.

There are two legitimate and different concerns regarding music. The first is "musical style." The second is "musical message."

This may be tough for you and me to accept, but there is, by and large, no morality—or immorality—to particular musical styles. Rock is not immoral, and classical is not moral. Country is not immoral, and jazz is not moral.

Regardless of your or your daughter's particular taste, I encourage you to request a *balance* of musical styles. Play a variety of music on the stereo in your house. Take her to the symphony. When you're in the car together, let her choose the radio stations. If you can't stand it or you think you might be getting carsick, respectfully ask if it would be okay to change the music.

We did tell our girls that, even though most musical styles are amoral, some music is more calming than others. We said that if the girls "had" to go to sleep or wake up to music, classical was their only choice. We did some battle with this, but eventually we reached an agreement. (Again, good luck with this one.)

As you already know, "musical messages" can be immoral. The greatest gift to you in this area is contemporary Christian music. Except for the extremes you find in secular music, there's enough variety in contemporary Christian musical styles to assuage any appetite. What will be missing will be the lyrics that promote everything you don't believe in.

Handling money

When was the last time you heard a dad complaining that his teenager "just doesn't appreciate the value of a dollar"? Yesterday? Me, too.

During the summer of 1967, when I was 19 years old, I cranked up my courage and asked a 21-year-old girl to dinner. Even though I was trying to save all my hard-earned money for my next college semester, I decided to take Jezebel (not her real name) to the most expensive restaurant in the area. When you're 19, you need to go the extra mile to impress an older woman.

Jezebel knew I was working to pay for school. On the way to dinner, I talked about how tough it was for me to earn enough during the summer to make a serious dent in tuition costs. But when the waitress came to take our order, Jezebel almost knocked me off my chair. She selected the most expensive entrée on the menu. In fact, there was a fine-print notation under the "Salads" section that read, "Roquefort dressing, $1.00 additional." And Jezebel ordered the Roquefort dressing.

It was a short night. I had to report to the construction site early the next morning in order to put in a few extra hours to cover Jezebel's thoughtlessness. Later, I heard that the following semester she met a lovely guy named Ahab, and that was the last I heard of her. Good luck, Ahab.

You can start teaching your daughter about money and its value when she's quite young. Teach her that there are only three uses for money: spending, saving, and giving. Show her, by your own example, how this works and why each of these uses is important: Spending is for living today, saving is for living tomorrow, and giving is the best way for money to make everyone—giver *and* recipient—happy.

Show your girl how to be frugal. Order water when you're out to dinner. Restaurants make a killing on drinks, so let them do it on the backs of dads who haven't read this book. Make a game out of coupon shopping at the grocery store.

Help your daughter to be creative in finding ways of making money. You can find books at your local bookstore that will offer useful ideas. Once she has begun collecting money of her own, show her how much to spend, save, and give.

If you're in the kind of financial condition that makes it possible for you to give your daughter all the money she needs, be careful. Give her the joy of investing her own money in something important to her. You'll be amazed at how much more she'll appreciate the things she buys with her own money than the things she's given.

Not long ago, my friend George told me the story of his daughter's bicycle. My guess is that George and his wife would have been in a financial position to painlessly buy Ginger a bike. Instead, however, he and his daughter developed a plan whereby they would split the cost. He told her, "You come up with $100, I'll match it, and we'll buy your bike." It wasn't easy, but Ginger worked and saved, and they bought the bike together. Actually, when he told me the story, George referred to this bike as "my daughter's immaculate bicycle." Any guesses why she takes that kind of care of her bike?

A year later, Ginger told her dad she'd like a special new tennis racket. When George and Ginger sat down to discuss the financial arrangements, Ginger finally told her dad to never mind. She'd use her mother's tennis racket!

If your family lives month to month and just keeps up with the bills, your daughter's active participation in the financial well-being of your family—as long as it's not overdone—will be a wonderful, character-building experience for her. Be sure you regularly express your gratitude for her help.

She'll understand at an early age what she'll need to know when she's married or on her own: the value of money. And because most American households depend on the woman to be the bookkeeper, you'll be giving your daughter's future family a wonderful gift.

Boys

No single dating—one boy, one girl, one car—until she's at least 16. Group dates or going to a school or church function before 16 are okay. Then after her sixteenth birthday, just know who the boys are. (See chapter 3.)

Over the years, dads have asked me about this hard-and-fast, 16-year-old rule. "Some girls are mature enough at 14, and some aren't ready until they're 18," they suggest. Of course, that's absolutely true. It's no different from our state "arbitrarily" deciding that, at 16, your daughter is ready to drive a car or that, at 18, she's ready to vote in a national election. Nonetheless, those are the laws.

My suggestion is that even if your daughter is mature enough to go out on a single date when she's 14, waiting two years won't inflict any permanent damage on her psyche. Make her wait. And if she's not ready at 16, don't push her into it. Let her wait until she's comfortable and, therefore, ready to tackle it on her own.

Perhaps the most frequent question I get on this subject is, "What if I just don't like the boy who wants to take out my daughter?"

If that's your question, please listen to what I'm about to say as carefully as you would if your life depended on it. First, you treat this boy's relationship with your daughter the same as you have any other friendship of hers from the time she was small. (See "Selecting friends" above.) Your success in building a relationship with your daughter based on open conversation, affection, and discipline will serve you very, very well once boys begin to appear on the scene.

Second, the interviewing process will have a natural sifting effect on the universe of boys willing to meet with you before courting your daughter. Remembering that you are *not* interviewing in order to decide whether your daughter can or can't see this boy—every boy passes—the process itself will fix most of your unsuitability concerns.

Finally, your high level of involvement in your daughter's friendships will have a powerful influence for good in the lives of those young people. This way your daughter won't be the only positive influence in the lives of her friends who haven't had the luxury your girl has had—growing up with a dad like you!

Get involved in the process. This is not a spectator sport.

Curfew

Curfew time should not be a hard-and-fast rule. Every situation creates its own be-home-by times. Just be sure you've established that time and that she always calls if she can't make it by that time. It may make you feel you're doing a good thing to require that your daughter always be the first one home out of her group of friends, but for her, it will become an unnecessary and counterproductive source of embarrassment. Don't die on this hill.

Smoking and alcohol

Rule number one is that there's no way you can enforce any guidelines here that are inconsistent with your own behavior. If you try it, she'll call your hand, and she has a right to.

I know that within Christian circles, there are honest differences of opinion regarding these issues, but let me take a run at them. Smoking is stupid. Ask anyone who smokes or has smoked. The vast majority of smokers will tell you they smoke for reasons other than the pure enjoyment(?!) of sucking blue smoke into their lungs. If your daughter starts to smoke, and this one's hard to hide, don't go crazy. Your overreaction will make the situation worse. Instead, talk to her. Listen to her. Pour on the verbal and physical affection. Talk to her in unemotional tones about the certainty of smoking's physical damage to her body.

If her smoking persists, you may want to find a Christian counselor who can help you discover ways to get through to your girl. (If you have no idea where to find a counselor, I suggest you call the Minirth-Meier New Life Clinics at 800-NEW-LIFE. They have more than 100 clinics around the country.)

Alcohol is about two things: the law and association. First, in every state, there are laws making underage drinking illegal. Don't allow your daughter to break those rules, even in your home. Second, alcohol and teenagers is about association—who they're hanging out with, peer pressure, and being cool.

Here's a case where "consequences" are your ally. Your daily newspaper will tell about people dying on the streets from using alcohol. If you live in a big city, you'll find an article every day. If you live in a rural area, it may be once a month. In any case, make certain your daughter understands the potential perils of alcohol abuse.

Having said that, let me encourage you not to let alcohol be an issue that destroys your relationship. Find a balance. In too many Christian homes, this becomes a needless sticking point—a major source of conflict. Do everything you can to steer clear of this. Above all, talk about it without raising your voice. Don't give her a "reason" for escaping, like a dad who's unreasonable and inflexible.

And Finally . . .

Never stop working on yourself. If the truth would be known, you and I are constantly doing battle with appropriate versus inappropriate behavior. As you work on improving yourself, tell your daughter about the tough challenges you're facing. Your openness will give her permission to let you in on her own "growing edges" and allow you to provide encouragement and help.

BUILDER'S CHECKLIST

1. *Speak the "finished product" to your daughter:* By saying kind or complimentary things to your daughter or about other children in her presence, you can clearly communicate the value you place on certain qualities.

2. *Correct conduct is a by-product of something else:* Protection, conversation, affection, correction, laughter, and faith should precede an emphasis on conduct.

3. *Make sure the guidelines are clearly defined:* Whatever they are, make certain your daughter understands the "rules." Don't surprise her with midcourse corrective "slaps." They won't work.

4. *Remember that conversation is still the key:* Your ability to talk through conduct issues, explaining why you've decided to set certain guidelines, will help to keep your home free from outbreaks of hostility. Having said that, however, if you decide to hold the line on certain conduct-related issues, don't expect your daughter to applaud your every decision. And when she doesn't, that's okay.

PART THREE

Gentlemen, we have our

Assignments

CHAPTER TEN

A quick look inside: *The guy from the city inspector's office*

"What lies behind us and what lies before us are tiny matters compared to what lies within us."

OLIVER WENDELL HOLMES

We've been talking about the ingredients necessary to build a daughter successfully. How well are you doing? You may only be starting with a tiny girl. You have almost everything to look forward to. Or you may be well on your way with a daughter who is growing tall and strong.

Let me ask you again, how well are you doing?

During the summers of 1966, 1967, and 1968, I worked for Richard Whitmer & Sons, a Chicago-area building contractor. Because Whitmer had decided that his would be a small company, I was his only full-time employee. When he landed large projects, he would bring in subcontractors to do the additional work. But for the most part, it was just Dick Whitmer and me.

As an 18-year-old boy, working for Whitmer gave me a love for construction. And we—Dick, mostly—did it all . . . pouring concrete, masonry, framing, welding, electrical, plumbing, and trim work. I had never labored so hard in my life, but I experienced the thrill of working, finishing, then standing back and actually seeing what I had helped to build. It was a feeling I never outgrew.

Of course, construction is filled with dangerous and even potentially deadly situations. Nearly every day, I'd do something to myself—bang my head on the scaffolding, drop a sheet of plywood on my foot, or skin my arm on something. Fortunately, I never did battle with any power tools.

When Dick would hear me say "ouch" or moan about something,

he'd always ask if he could see it. It was probably an insurance-company thing. I'd show him the injury, and he would say, "Hey, if it grows back, we don't worry about it."

Of all the on-the-job injuries I had, I most hated getting wood splinters in my hands. Give me a sharp bang on the head with a pro-truding 2-by-10, but please, please don't give me a sliver. When Dick would ask to see it, I'd have to show him. Recognizing what I had buried in my tender finger, Dick would pull out his large and well-worn pocket knife, flip it open, "disinfect" it by wiping it across his work pants, and cut out the splinter. I had to tough it out like in the old cowboy movies, when a victim's compadres would remove a bullet from his leg. Sometimes tears would trickle down my cheek, but I'd never make a sound.

Someone Is Watching

Because it was usually just the two of us on these building sites, I remember thinking, *How fun. Dick and I can do just about anything we want on the job. We can do work on this building, button the job up, then get on with the next one . . . just like constructing a fort in the backyard with my friends, only much better.*

This was before I knew anything about building inspectors. Every city and county in America has them. Chicago, where I lived, had lots and lots of them. Their job is to visit construction sites and approve the contractor's work at the completion of every stage. The next time you visit an unfinished building, look for the building permit posted in a prominent place. You'll see the initials of the various inspectors who, by their approval, gave the contractor permission to move on.

If an inspector found something he didn't judge to be "code," or if he was just having a bad day, he would make us go back and fix it before moving on. Those delays were not only frustrating, but, according to Dick, they could also be extremely costly.

I came to deeply respect—and fear—the power of the building inspector.

Who's Going to Inspect Our Work?

We started this book with an understanding that "building" a daughter is one of the most wonderful and challenging "projects" you and I will ever face. It's filled with lots of hard work coupled with the joy of "standing back" to see what we've built. It also has its share of dangers—bumps, scrapes, and splinters—along the way.

> God knows my "work" is a reflection of my character.

But who inspects *our* work? To whom do we answer for the quality of our performance?

King David wrote something sobering about the process of inspection:

> *Search me, O God, and know my heart;*
> *test me and know my anxious thoughts.*
> *See if there is any offensive way in me,*
> *and lead me in the way everlasting.*
> Psalm 139: 23–24

Did you catch *what* the Inspector is inspecting? He's not checking my work. He's inspecting *me*. God knows my "work" is a reflection of my character. If my heart meets "code," my work—as a person or a dad—will be acceptable to Him.

C'mon, You Can Say It

In a sense, this chapter is a footnote, because, instead of helping you with one more technique toward properly building your girl, it's about you and me—the builders.

Are you alone right now? If not, I want you to either clear the room or go somewhere by yourself. In chapter 2, we admitted, out loud, that we are quitters. Well, I've got another one. And since this is just between you and me, I don't want anyone else to hear you.

I want you to say the following at least loud enough so you can hear the sound of your own voice. I'm serious. In fact, while I'm writing this, I'll say it out loud, too, so you won't be saying it all by yourself.

Are you ready? Is the room clear? Okay, say the following in an audible voice. No fair whispering.

"I need inspection."

Did you say it? Good.

Before you and I have a chance to be effective fathers, we have to become complete men. And before we can become complete, we have to admit what we just admitted. We must admit that we're *not* complete and could use some regular internal inspection.

Beyond Technique and Style

Here's a pretty sobering thought: Your success as a dad will have far more to do with who you are than with how well you're able to do certain things with and for your daughter. Ultimately, she will learn more by watching you than by listening to you—more from your example than from your teaching techniques.

This means you could be a perfect father "performer." You could understand your need to protect your daughter; you could be a brilliant conversationalist; you could learn to be tender and a tough disciplinarian; you could laugh with your girl; you could faithfully take her to church; and you could establish crystal-clear guidelines for conduct. You could do all these things and be a colossal failure.

My little brother, Dan, was a wrestler. As a high schooler, he was quite small, so since his school didn't offer competitive horse racing, he found the one sport that provided a significant opportunity for smaller boys. One particular year, the school bought new uniforms for the team. My brother recalls how excited all the athletes were and how good they looked in their new outfits . . . as good as anyone could look in a wrestling uniform.

However, the first wrestling meet of the year was a disaster. Those handsome young men in their chic and stylish wardrobes were getting stuck—pinned—left and right. Halfway through the meet, the hard-driving and sometimes overzealous coach called the boys together for a little talk.

"Men," he began, "I like your new uniforms. I really do. You look terrific." Setting up the youngsters for the kill, he continued, "But if you'll check out the scoreboard, you'll notice that you're lookin' pretty and gettin' beat!"

The lesson is clear: As dads, you and I may find ourselves more concerned about visible tactics—to-do lists—for effective fathering, but if we forget that our true success will come only from what's inside, we're destined for predictably heartbreaking consequences.

Please, No More Lists!

I've already given you more lists of things to do than you've ever seen in one place, so let me boil everything down to just two final things you need to keep in mind to be ready for inspection.

Your personal walk with Christ

Only God makes dads complete. The apostle Paul said it this way: "In Him [Jesus Christ] you have been made complete" (Col. 2:10, NASB).

Simple, isn't it? For you to be a complete man—and dad—Jesus

Christ offers you the gift of "completeness." Wholeness. Comfort. And He does this every day. From the sleepless nights when you first bring your daughter home to the terror you feel about turning her loose, God promises His wisdom and peace.

Begin your day on your knees. Buy a devotional book, and let it be your daily road map. Thank God for His goodness. Confess your sins. Pray for courage to think and do the right thing. Pray for your daughter. Ask God to make you His worthy representative in your workplace and to your family.

Do this every single day. Have a place that reminds you of your time alone with God—a quiet spot that becomes the special location for your private meeting.

Find someone to walk with you

Several years ago, I had a long and wonderfully memorable conversation with my friend Dr. Neil Warren. Dr. Warren is a highly successful author, speaker, and counselor. He told me that when a new client comes to him, he always makes the same request in their first session: "Tell me about your three closest friends."

If the new client is a woman, the answer is usually quick in coming. Often, the woman will describe more than three friends, then explain how difficult it is to narrow the list to just three.

If the new client is a man, there's often a long pause, followed by the question, "What, exactly, do you mean by *best* friend?"

Let's face it, most men aren't adept at building close friendships. Sure, there are guys we enjoy being with, watching the playoffs with, hunting or fishing with . . . but "close" friends? What, exactly, do I mean by close friends?

In his landmark bestseller, *The Man in the Mirror*, Patrick Morley says it this way: "God's Word teaches us how to stand firm in the faith and to guard against falling away . . . yet, men do fall away because they don't have to answer to anyone for their behavior and beliefs. The answer—the missing link—is accountability."

Find a group of friends, men to whom you can be regularly answerable for each of the key areas of your life. Don't try to go it alone.

In his book, Morley tells the story of Lawrence Taylor, the New York Giant linebacker who, in his prime, was one of the most skillful and ferocious the game had ever seen. But in 1988, after being suspended by the National Football League for violating its substance-abuse policy, Taylor was quoted in *The New York Times:* "God, I didn't mean for it to happen. I wish it hadn't, but I made a bad decision and I'll have to pay for it. . . . I really wasn't allowing the Giants to help me. I wasn't allowing my wife to help me. I was doing it by myself and trying to make it happen by myself because I wanted to say I could do it on my own. It doesn't work that way. Boy, I found that out."

> *Find a group of friends, men to whom you can be regularly answerable for each of the key areas of your life.*

Find a few men—three to five—who will be willing to meet with you *regularly.* Commit to total honesty and confidentiality. Don't let the group meet unless everyone can be there. Tell each other about the victories and the defeats in your personal life, your family, and your work life.

> *As iron sharpens iron,*
> *so one man sharpens another.*
> Proverbs 27:17

Read books as a group—*The Man in the Mirror* would be a great one to start with—and pray together.

> *Confess your sins to each other and pray for each other*

so that you may be healed.
The prayer of a righteous man is powerful and effective.
James 5:16

If you maintain a daily time with God and commit yourself to a handful of friends, I can promise your life will be inspectable. And because of God's grace and mercy, you'll "pass code," ready to move ahead with the big job of successfully building your daughter into a well-balanced, godly, and complete woman.

Hey, good news! I just checked your "building permit," and God's signature is on it.

BUILDER'S CHECKLIST

1. *Prepare for inspection:* Every construction project—and man— has to face inspection.

2. *Watch your example:* Success in building a daughter is more dependent on your own life than on your ability to follow fathering techniques.

3. *Tend to your insides:* A dad's inner growth must include time spent alone with God.

4. *Establish accountability:* Joining with a small group of friends, meeting to be accountable to each other, may be the most important thing you can do to stay on track as an effective father.

5. *Say this closing prayer:* If you feel you need to recommit yourself to "being" rather than just "doing," you're welcome to pray the following:

"Dear God, I admit that without You, my life doesn't pass Your code. But I thank You for Your grace. I thank You that through

Your mercy, I have a way to pass Your inspection. I renew my commitment to You as my Lord and Savior, and I promise to never forget that from this moment on, I can tackle the job of building my daughter with the strength of Your love and power. In Jesus' name, amen."

For "special" dads: *Stepdads, long-distance dads, and single dads*

I was having breakfast with my friend Skip. He was updating me on his life, and I was filling him in on mine. When I told him I was writing a book for dads, he asked me an important question: "What are you saying to dads in special situations like me — blended-family dads, stepdads, adoptive dads, or single dads?"

My first thought was that most of this book ought to fit, regardless of a dad's particular situation, but I promised I would go back and carefully read it through one more time, just to be sure. Then, as an afterthought, I suggested that perhaps I should ask Skip, and other dads who are in one of those special situations, to review the manuscript and meet together to discuss it. From the responses those men gave me, I offer a few comments that may be especially helpful to dads in such families.

Blended-Family Dads

If your family includes your wife's daughter, the most critical issue you'll face is earning the right to *be* the dad. This girl is not your own, and she'll often feel free to obey you or not as she chooses. "You're not my dad" will bring discussions, and especially confrontational situations, to a speedy and painful end.

There's only one person who can give you official "permission" to be the dad, and that's the girl's mother — your wife. That means you and she need to regularly confer on issues related to your daughter and agree on specific strategies. All this must happen before you reveal those policies to your stepdaughter so that when you do, your wife will back you up.

If your stepdaughter joined your family at age 12 or 13, you may need to ask your wife to take part in some of the fathering chores. For example, if you choose to interview boys (chapter 3) prior to your stepdaughter's going out on a date, your wife will probably need to do it, either alone or with you. She has the most history with her daughter, so she may need to take the lead.

Help your wife to understand that as she interacts with her daughter alone, her support of you will make or break your ability to be the dad—or one of the dads—for this girl.

One of the dads told us that through years of broken promises and neglect, his stepdaughter had learned to mistrust her biological father. What her father *said* had no bearing on what he *did*. Through years of trustworthiness, my friend had "just begun" to win this girl's trust. He stressed the importance of patience and understanding.

Just a temporary bridge

Are you familiar with the temporary, floating bridges the military often uses to span a river quickly? Unlike permanent bridges made with lots of steel and concrete, these connections between two riverbanks can be assembled in a matter of hours.

However, unlike permanent spans, temporary bridges are more susceptible to destruction—raging rivers or guerrilla attacks can render them useless in a short time.

> *The relationship "bridge" between you and your stepdaughter is not a permanent bridge.*

The relationship "bridge" between you and your stepdaughter is *not* a permanent bridge. When your family was blended and she came along with the deal, it happened relatively quickly. You weren't there when she was born. You didn't change her diapers or teach her to walk. One day she wasn't there; the next she appeared.

This relationship is "temporary." Like the military bridge, it can be easily broken. You must remember that yesterday's passable bridge will not necessarily be there tomorrow. To insure a safe crossing, the relationship will need constant maintenance.

How old is she?

The younger your stepdaughter was when she came to live with you, the more your relationship with her will be similar to dealing with your own child. The older she is, the more careful and deliberate you'll need to be.

Conversation is still the key. Talk to her—a lot. Let this girl know who you are, and give her a chance to reciprocate. Don't force this by interrogating her; invite it by being transparent yourself. As she reaches her teenage years, let her in on your ideas about being a dad—the why's and the strategies. If they make sense to her, ask her for the green light to be her coach, and hold her accountable. Help *her* to paint the picture of the "finished product." If you do this, she'll be more open to your protection and discipline.

Careful affection

After reading this manuscript, one of the dads expressed his concerns related to affection (chapter 5), especially as his girls changed from children into women. He told our group that he has two daughters in his home, one a stepdaughter and the other his biological child. He told us how much he loves both girls, but he expressed the subtle differences between them. In every girl's life, there will come a time when she becomes aware of her own need for modesty around her dad. This time will likely arrive sooner with your stepdaughter than with your biological daughter. Honor her need for privacy.

He went on to tell us that most of the principles in *She Calls Me Daddy* were appropriate for both his daughters, but then he gave the following caution: "When it comes to physical affection, I'm more cautious with my stepdaughter. Somehow in the deepest recess of my heart, I *know* she's not my child. So I'm more careful physically. I'm very open with my verbal affection, but I let her take the lead with bear hugs and kisses."

Her other dad

Every blended-family situation has its own special conditions. Yours is no exception. If you're comfortable speaking to your stepdaughter's biological dad, I encourage you to make occasional contact, even by phone. Such calls can be important, especially as they relate to the task of effectively fathering this girl. Honor him by letting him know you want his input. However, don't do this without the full knowledge and consent of your wife and daughter. This is about cooperation, not conspiracy.

You may even suggest that her dad read this book, giving the two of you a basis for discussing specific ideas and approaches. The more you eliminate the opportunities for your girl to "play both ends against the middle," the more effective you'll both be. And the more you can contribute to a good relationship between your stepdaughter and her biological father, the healthier she'll be.

A volunteer dad and daughter

My first job right out of college was in full-time youth work. For seven years, Bobbie and I got to know hundreds of high schoolers. One thing that struck me early on was that all the kids we worked with *chose* to be involved in our club meetings and camps. They were all free agents, volunteers. When they wanted to meet with us, they did. But the moment they didn't want to be part of our program, they left.

I couldn't afford to make any assumptions about those relationships. I couldn't take the kids for granted. I had to constantly earn the right to be involved in their lives.

It's been almost 30 years since we first met some of those teenagers. They've grown up. Lots of them have families of their own. But as we've stayed in contact with some of them, we've come to realize that we were able to do this because we weren't coaches, parents, teachers, or ministers. The kids weren't players, children, students, or parishioners. We were all volunteers—the teenagers and us. We chose to be connected to each other.

Your role as a stepdad will be a lot like that. You have chosen to love this girl, and your hope is that she'll choose to love you, too.

Long-Distance Dads

One of the dads in our group was his daughter's biological father, but she lived with her mother in another city. He told us how painful it was to not have regular contact with her and how he missed seeing her every day. The most significant thing he emphasized was the need for regular "word touchings."

When Bobbie and I were falling in love, we had what we thought was a real problem. She lived in Washington, D.C., and I was at school in Indiana. How could we possibly build this relationship when we lived so far apart?

Now, looking back on that time, we're both grateful for the distance. Was it *better* than being together? Probably not. But the miles gave us the chance to slowly but surely introduce each other to our deepest thoughts and feelings—in writing.

If you're a long-distance dad, even though you don't have the

luxury of physically hugging your daughter every day, touch her
with your words regularly. I *really* want to say "daily" here, but I
don't want to freak you out!

I have a friend who bought his daughter a fax machine, and he
pays for the extra phone line. I've seen some of the late-night faxes,
hand scrawled on a single piece of paper from his daughter: "I've
had a wild day—two tests and a paper—and I'm about to go to bed,
but I just wanted to tell you I love you, Dad. Love, Amy." I've seen
notes from him: "The meeting with the Acme vice president went
great. I think we might get the order. It would sure help me make my
sales quota. I love you and I miss you, Amy. Love, Dad."

We know a dad who bought his daughter a subscription to the
Internet, and they send "notes" to each other almost every day.

And what do you say every day? Just the news: what your day was
like; whom you met with; what you did. These (almost) daily word
touchings don't need to be filled with mushy things. Just provide regular updates to keep her appraised. And every once in a while, shoot
her a joke or a cartoon you found in the paper. Laughing together
isn't as fun long distance as it is when you're together, but it can still
help to seal the bond.

Although the bridge between you and your long-distance daughter
is probably more permanent than the military span I talked about
earlier with stepdads, there are times when it won't "feel" that way.
But you can do something to keep the bridge strong; you've got to do
it constantly: Communicate!

Suck it up

Be careful with the things you tell your daughter about what's going
on between you and her mother. One of the dads in our group
summed up what he does when he's talking to his daughter about
her mother: "I refuse to get involved in negative conversation about

my ex-wife. I tell myself, *Bob, don't do this. It will not help your daughter to get caught in the middle. You might think you have the right to slam your ex, but don't do it. It won't help a thing. Just suck it up."*

In fact, as much as you can, affirm your daughter's relationship with her mother. In most cases, your girl will be better for it.

Single Dads

You have a tough job. Never having been a young girl yourself, there will be times when you're mystified by what's going on with your daughter. If you've been widowed and you really *are* doing this fathering thing alone, pray for adult women who will befriend your girl. Church is the best place to "find" such women: the wife of the youth director, the mother of a friend she meets, a Sunday school teacher. Such women will save your life.

> *Speak kind words about your ex-wife in your daughter's presence.*

If you're divorced, encourage your daughter to build a solid relationship with her mother. Speak kind words about your ex-wife in your daughter's presence. This is the only mother your girl has, and if you can enhance their relationship, do it.

Lighten up

As a single dad, you may be tempted to lean too heavily on your daughter emotionally. Be careful. Resist the temptation to "use" her to meet your own relational needs. Don't force her to grow up too quickly just because you don't have an adult companion. Find a small group of men to walk through this with you. (See chapter 10.) They'll be a big help.

It's Never Too Late

Many "special dads" live with tremendous regrets. If you're one of those, you know that dwelling on the "if only's" can bury you. Yes, you've made some choices that have unalterably affected your role as your daughter's daddy. This isn't how you expected your life to turn out.

However, let me encourage you to spend less time looking back and more time looking ahead. Someone has described the past as hardened concrete and the future as wet cement. Rather than filling your mind with what you could have or should have done, focus on what you can do from this point on.

Tell your daughter you're sorry about how your decisions have made her growing-up more of a challenge. But promise her that, starting now, you want to recommit yourself to being the best dad— step, long-distance, or single—you can possibly be.

It's *never* too late to start being a better daddy.

QUESTIONS FOR DISCUSSION

Chapter One

1. *Now, that's funny:* The book opens with a story about a Jockey-shorts-clad Robert getting caught at midnight in the living room by his daughter's friend. What funny story can you remember about your fathering experience? If your daughter is too young for you to have any funny stories yet, can you remember one from your own childhood?

2. *What gets you out of bed on a Saturday morning?:* You may not be into building projects, but what would get you out of bed early on a Saturday morning? Can you identify with how motivating it feels to look forward to something you really enjoy doing?

3. *The big day:* Recall the events leading up to and including the birth of your daughter. Did you want a girl, or were you a little—or a lot—disappointed that she wasn't a boy? Why?

4. *This particular project:* Why are you reading this book? Take a moment to reflect on what you would like to "accomplish" by spending some time reading and thinking about your relationship with your daughter. Are there any specific goals you'd like to set?

5. *You're the only daddy she'll ever have:* How does it make you feel to read that statement? Why?

Chapter Two

1. *Underestimating:* Remember a time when you underestimated how long something was going to take to finish. Did you complete the project? If so, what got you through to the end? What project do you have going on right now that needs to get finished?

2. *'Fessing up:* When was the last time you were so exasperated with your daughter that you felt like "quitting"?

3. *Not quitting:* Recall a situation when you were tempted to quit—but you finished instead. How did it feel when you didn't give in to the temptation?

Chapter Three

1. *Protection equals value:* Besides family and friends, name several of your things that you consider valuable. What measures do you take to protect them?

2. *The seesaw:* Explain the way physical and emotional protection change during your daughter's lifetime. Where is your daughter today regarding her need for each? Does she need a lot or a little?

3. *What's stopping you?:* What keeps you from effectively carrying out your duty to protect your daughter? Why?

4. *Balance:* What are some examples where a dad's protection of his daughter could be overdone? Underdone? What can you do to strike a balance?

5. *The interview:* What is the purpose of interviewing your daughter's dates when she turns 16?

Chapter Four

1. *Powerful trouble:* Recall a situation when your words got you in trouble.

2. *Teaching conversation:* What benefits accrue to your daughter when you teach her how to carry on a conversation with you? Other adults? Boys?

3. *Getting started:* Given the current age of your daughter, what kinds of things could you do this week to improve her conversation skills?

4. *Crown jewel?:* Why do you think Robert referred to conversation as the "crown jewel"?

Chapter Five

1. *Physical affection:* What are some examples of nondramatic but still meaningful touchings? What can you do with your daughter—what kinds of games could you play, for example—to increase the frequency of physical contact?

2. *Verbal affection:* Recall, from your own childhood, the memory of someone who spoke kind words to you. How do you feel about that person today? What are some moments you could capture to verbally "touch" your daughter?

3. *More deposits, please:* What can you do to improve your balance in your daughter's "account"?

Chapter Six

1. *All yeses:* How does our culture promote the idea that yes is good and no is bad?

2. *Punishment:* How were you punished as a child? Who did the punishing?

3. *Swift, painful, and fair discipline:* Do you agree that discipline should be swift, painful, and fair? Why or why not?

4. *Discipline is its own reward:* What does the preceding statement mean to you? How could it be applied to your own experience as a person in addition to your role as a dad?

Chapter Seven

1. *The Sea Cloud Sport Boat:* When have you been hoodwinked by a certain expectation, only to find the reality far different?

2. *Laughing on purpose:* Is there enough laughter in your home? What do you do to bring laughter into your daughter's life?

3. *A little candor:* Are you fun to live with? On a scale of 1 (total bore) to 10 (fun guy), what number would you give yourself? Why?

4. *A little more candor:* On the same scale of 1 to 10, what score would your daughter give you? Why?

Chapter Eight

1. *Take some time:* Go back over the list of ways to build godly character in your daughter from the Builder's Checklist on pages 158–59.

2. *Check them out:* Which of the things on the checklist have you already done? Which would you like to start doing? What things would you add to the list?

3. *Goals to shoot for:* This list should be the foundation of a faith-building strategy for you and your daughter. Don't be overwhelmed by the size of the list; just pick a few, and see how much fun this can be.

Chapter Nine

1. *Your experience:* What kind of discipline did you receive as a child? How do you feel about it now? Why?

2. *Order?:* Do you agree or disagree with Robert's reasons for putting this chapter at the end of the list of seven things to do as a father? Why?

3. *By-product:* What are some examples of how "fixing" something you're dealing with related to an earlier chapter could solve a conduct problem?

4. *Finished product:* How can you "speak to the goal you're attempting to reach" with your daughter? What kinds of things could you begin doing right away to "paint this picture" for your girl?

5. *Unusual allies:* How can negative consequences and positive rewards be good "helpers" in your task of teaching your daughter proper conduct?

6. *What do you think?:* As you review the list of issues related to conduct, ask yourself these questions: What do I agree with? What do I disagree with? Why?

7. *Work to do:* Based on your answers to the previous question, what do you need to begin working on with your daughter?

8. *Being liked is not as important as doing what's right:* How do you feel about the preceding statement? How would it help you when the going gets tough?

Chapter Ten

1. *Codes:* How might a community look if there were no building codes? Are you glad—even if you're a contractor!—for inspectors and codes? Why or why not?

2. *Your example:* In your own words, why does your ability as a father depend more on who you are than on how you employ certain fathering techniques?

3. *Your time of quiet reflection and prayer:* How are you doing in the disciplines of quiet times and prayer? How can you sharpen this area of your personal life?

4. *To whom do you answer?:* Do you have an "accountability group"? If not, list three men you think might be interested in doing this with you. Then call them and set up a meeting.

Other Faith and Family Strengtheners
From Robert Wolgemuth

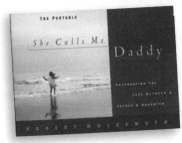

The Portable She Calls Me Daddy

This wonderful little book celebrates the love between a father and daughter. Whether she's a toddler or a teen, *The Portable She Calls Me Daddy,* is full of practical nuggets of advice for busy dads to show their daughters how much they are loved and cherished. Discover how to explore your faith together and show her the meaning of integrity, responsibility, and maturity. Paperback.

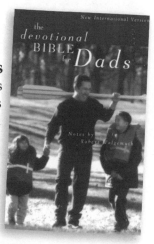

The Devotional Bible for Dads

The greatest legacy any man can have is his children. But in a society that measures success in terms of money and power, where can a Christian man find encouragement to be a better father? *The Devotional Bible for Dads* offers a no-nonsense resource that can encourage men in their own walk with God and help them pass the torch of faith on to their children. Full of insights from well-known and successful Christian dad, Robert Wolgemuth, this Bible offers a variety of study helps to enable dads to maximize the quality of their relationships with their families. Available in both paperback and hardcover.

Look for these special books in your Christian bookstore.

If you are interested in having **Robert Wolgemuth** speak to your church, organization, conference, or special event, please contact:

Interact Speaker's Bureau